You
Can Get
There From
Here

You Can Get There From Here

Life Lessons on Growth and Self-Discovery for the Black Woman

by D. Anne Browne

BRYANT & DILLON PUBLISHERS
ORANGE, NEW JERSEY

ACKNOWLEDGMENTS

The quotations that precede each chapter and selected sections were taken from *The Art of War* (by Sun Tzu, as translated by Thomas Cleary) and *Tao Te Ching: The Classic Book of Integrity and The Way* (by Lao Tzu, based on the recently discovered Ma-Wang-Tui manuscripts).

Cover and text design by Laurie Williams/A Street Called Straight

Cover photograph courtesy of Vincent S. Barronette, II

Library of Congress Cataloging-in-Publication Data
Brown, D. Anne
1. You can get there from here 2. Self Help 3. Women's Studies
(A Bryant & Dillon Book)

95-77774
ISBN 0-9638672-6-1

Printed in the United States of America
10 9 8 7 6 5 4 3 2

To Stan and Betsey Heuisler for paving the way.

To Vivian Mason for knowing the way.

To Elfrieda Queen for seeing the way.

To my sister Carolyn for embracing motherhood and sharing it with me.

To Rick Flichman for wanting to be a role model.

To Janet Adams, whose love of children will not go unrewarded.

To Chenal Alford, II, for being the stimulation for my being.

To Vernon Simms for recognizing the greater good.

To Myron Wickham for making time stand still.

To all of my real friends who have helped me to find my way.

To everyone who believes in the magic of being a child.

Contents

To the Reader

This book is the result of many years of informal interviews, rap sessions, and confidence sharing between me and the Black men and women with the interest, courage, and desire to contribute to my learning process. Without them, *You Can Get There From Here* would not have been possible. The text contained here is not the result of a clinical study or medical evaluation. Rather, it is a testament to the profound wisdom that flourishes in the minds of common men (and women).

About the Self-Surveys

As a layperson and the author of this book, it is not my intention to offer the reader medical advice, psychological counseling, or clinical diagnosis. What is intended here is to provide a stimulus for an open dialogue between Black men and women so that the healing process for them will continue. To assist with that process, ten statements and/or questions have been included at the end of each chapter. The idea behind those statements is threefold. First, they have been included to give you a general overview of the preceding chapter. Second, they have been included to serve as food for thought. Third, they have been included to invite your introspection and to stimulate self-awareness. These statements or "self-surveys" are not questionnaires. So, there is no such thing as an "appropriate" response to them, except for the response that is most positive and appropriate to *you*. The self-surveys are not test questions.

There are no right or wrong answers and good or bad responses to them.

The self-surveys are intended not only to reinforce the theme of each chapter, but also to encourage free thinking and open discussion without bias, prejudgment, or fear. Their ultimate goal is to bring out your best thoughts and to motivate you to translate those thoughts into actions that promote achieving your highest human potential and greatest good.

Forword

Somewhere between trying to conform to the norms of a dominant White society and understanding the roots of conflicts (and their resolutions) within the Black culture, a terrible thing happened to Black women. They became contaminated. As they basked in the afterglow of White cultural acceptance, they became displaced members of their own culture. The sociological and psychological toxins that they permitted to infiltrate their systems have made them oblivious to their own identities as Black women. These Black women do not seem to know who they are or where they belong. The good news is that not all Black women have been contaminated. The bad news is that enough contamination has occurred to upset the cultural balance. Those Black women who have allowed themselves to become devalued have been reduced to functioning as displaced persons with misplaced loyalties and allegiances. As a Black woman, I am certain that my "rightful place" in American society should not be based on the ideologies of a racist, narrow-minded, paranoid cross-section of society whose primary objective seems to be making me feel ashamed of who I am.

I would venture to guess that you could go into any Black neighborhood, ask any Black child to describe a typical middle-class White style of living, and find that such a description would be delivered with amazing accuracy. Even though that child never may have had exposure to that lifestyle, s/he may still be able to describe it to you in detail. On the other hand, you might travel to a White middle- or upper-class neighborhood and ask a White child the same questions about the lifestyles of Black people. The inaccuracies may astound you. There is an important reason for the difference between the "information" that each child has. Black children are constantly bombarded with a variety of images that glorify the White style of living. Television, magazines, and movies continually boast about the advantages of being White over being a person of any other race. The White child is taught to view him/herself as a member of an elite and powerful group. That training is reinforced by parents who endorse a particular style of living, schools that promote a particular course of thinking, and traditions that incorporate a particular method of action. White children are exposed to Blacks in a limited way. That exposure frequently does not accurately portray the lifestyles of Black people or the true roles that they play in society. White children are not reinforced for questioning the validity of racism or rewarded for acting outside of the traditional racial boundaries that have separated them from other races. And so, the cycle continues.

Who would have predicted that the people kidnapped from their homeland some 400 years ago would have produced generations of descendants with the drive, will, and genius to survive, excel, and evoke positive changes in a hostile White world? That is exactly what Black people have done. As unsung as we may be, Black people have become the heros and heroines that America has needed on countless occasions. We have achieved greatness in every field of endeavor and inspired greatness in others. That fact has been lost in the quagmire that we call racism. If we suppose that racism is nothing more than a collective effort by a dominant group to suppress a people, then it is imperative for Black people collectively to be certain of who they are. That knowledge is our only defense. Knowing the group to which you belong is important to the survival of that group. However, knowing who you are as an individual is necessary for your survival. That is the basis for *You Can Get There From Here.* It is not enough to recognize the effects that racism and prejudice have on the group as a whole. That recognition needs to be supplemented with an understanding of *why* such campaigns are effective against

xii

the individual. Each Black person is an individual member of a unique and wonderful culture. It is the collection of our individual actions that help to define who we are as a group because, like any chain, it is only as strong as its weakest link.

Being a Black woman in America is a truly unique position to hold. It has afforded me the opportunity to enjoy the cultural advantages of being what I am while defending my inalienable right to be who I am. Being a bronze-skinned, full-lipped, round-hipped woman is only part of who I am. It is only part of what Black women are. Unfortunately, not enough Black women seem to realize that. Black women are also inventors, intellectuals, and administrators. More important, Black women are the facilitators of the Black race. They can never be obsolete, because they are necessary for the survival of the race. What Black women teach their children is crucial to the survival of those children. What they share with one another is important to their individual survival. What Black women accept as fact about themselves and their culture is an important component of racial and cultural harmony. So, it stands to reason that a Black woman cannot possibly give complete love to anyone until she can love herself completely first. Without self-love, she cannot love others. Without self-awareness, she cannot clearly recognize the impact that others have on her life. Without self-knowledge, she cannot really know those persons who affect who she believes herself to be.

This book centers around the idea that the inner cultivation of Black women will lead to their outer resonance. It is based on the belief in the collective power associated with having achieved self-awareness and self-understanding. It is founded on the fundamental truth that self-understanding is necessary before the understanding of others can be possible.

I deliberately chose certain vehicles to help support that belief. The Asian form of philosophy known as Taoism has been injected throughout the book because the teachings of Tao provide strategies that are permeated with ideas that are essential to promoting an insightful exchange between those who seek knowledge and those who hold knowledge. The teachings of Tao encourage that initial thoughts be directed to inner cultivation without diminishing the validity of other forms of philosophical thought. The largest attraction of a work such as *Tao Te Ching and The Art of War* is that it is so applicable to modern circumstances and uniquely relevant to self-discovery and individual empowerment. For the purposes of this book, the messages are of far greater significance than the messenger.

It only seemed logical that a body of work devoted to self-awareness also include theories of individual motivation. Because we are nothing more and nothing less than what we believe ourselves to be, the doctrines found in "humanist" psychology help to provide reasonable explanations for why and when those beliefs occur. The humanist approach to behavior focuses on theories of motivation on individual abilities. Those theories are so basic in their premise that being a layperson did not retard my understanding of how they could be applied directly to the Black experience. The popular psychology and philosophy presented in *You Can Get There From Here* is meant to stimulate positive thinking in the reader. It is not an attempt to clinically diagnose or promote a "divide and conquer" attitude between groups of people.

If you are a Black woman, I cannot emphasize enough how important it is for you to focus on *reality*. Understandably, that term may mean different things to different people, but for you the realities of being a Black woman in America are the same no matter where you live, what your income, is or how much formal education you have acquired. The reality for you is that this country was not founded on the basis of real equality. The Constitution of the United States was not written for women or for Black

xiv

people. It is based on those ideals that its authors held for themselves. Fortunately for Black women, the language of the Constitution can be manipulated in their favor, because its authors lacked the foresight to anticipate its application to persons other than White men.

Introduction

America is often referred to as a "melting pot." It is viewed by many as a homogeneous mixture of peoples and cultures. It is considered by non-Americans as a vast land of plenty. The reality for Black people is that this place called America sprang forth from the seeds of revolution and was founded on the idea of supremacy—that is, a select group of people should reign over everyone else. Through the years, America has done its best to live up to the concept of supremacy. Every Black person in America has had some experience with this concept. The nature of our "arrival" to this country has been and continues to be an excuse to justify the atrocities and brutalities committed against us as a people. No amount of collective White guilt will change what has occurred or prevent it from continuing. That is something that Black Americans must ensure for themselves.

However, if supremacy were simply a matter of strength and fortitude, Black people have proven their supremacy. We have survived the beatings, the cross burnings, and the indentured servitude. If supremacy were simply a question of genius, Black people have proven their supremacy. We have applied our literary, scientific, and mathematical skills to areas previously uncharted with unprecedented genius. If supremacy were simply an issue of courage, Black people have proven their supremacy. We have fought in war time trenches and battled on peacetime home fronts. We have done all that was asked of us and submitted to what was demanded from us. We have met the criteria for supremacy no matter how varied its definition became. *We have nothing to prove to America.*

We do, however, seem to have plenty to prove to ourselves, because we do not reign supreme in our own minds. So, we must begin at the beginning. We must reject anything and everything that suggests, contends, or implies that we are lesser persons. We must eliminate the signs, symbols, and signals that portray us as worthless Americans and replace them with images that celebrate our citizenship and right to exist in this country as *no less than equals* to others. This book is meant to address some of the concerns that Black women have about themselves, their children, their mates, and their lives. Hopefully, it will help to open a positive and productive dialogue between them. Not all Black women are presented here. No one book could do that. Not all issues pertinent to the Black experience could be examined here. The concerns of Black people are too diverse and varied to be addressed in a single method of exploration. What the reader will find is a small representative sample of the general impact that Western thought can have on persons of African descent. Within that sample are examples of how adaptive, creative, and strong Black people can be without dismissing the self-destructive, maladaptive, and ignorant choices that they sometimes make.

karma
n. 1. Hinduism and Buddhism. The sum and consequences of a person's actions during the successive phases of his existence. 2. Fate; destiny.

CHAPTER ONE

What You Already Know

Understanding others is knowledge.
Understanding oneself is enlightenment.
Conquering others is power.
Conquering oneself is strength.

Knowledge is an essential component of power. Knowledge is an intangible force that dominates our behavior. Knowledge is not something that can be physically touched, smelled, or tasted, but its impact on us can most certainly be felt. How much and what we know about ourselves and our world contribute to how powerful we believe ourselves to be. Situations that make us feel powerless are not just those situations we feel are unavoidable or uncomfortable. We feel powerless when we believe that *we do not know how* to avoid or change those situations. Believing ourselves knowledgeable is what helps to make us feel secure about who we are and our ability to ensure the quality of life that we want. Believing ourselves knowledgeable helps to contribute to our feelings of self-empowerment.

Some of us believe that we know everything about something. Others of us believe that we know something about everything. There are even those of us who don't seem to believe that we know very much about anything. Still, the one thing that we all have in common (unless we were unfortunate enough to have been born with some medical disability) is that we have a sufficient enough knowledge of our surroundings to exist safely and harmoniously with other people. When our ability to correctly perceive or detect is intact, we are able to know such things as where our bodies are in space, when others are in our presence, or when the potential for danger is near. That knowledge is very basic, but without it we could not survive. For instance, if we did not know the difference between the red and green traffic lights, we could not cross an intersection or drive a car without causing harm to ourselves or to other people. If we did not know the difference between the symbol for the men's and ladies' rooms, we probably would not be able to use public rest rooms without causing ourselves and other people to feel uncomfortable.

The relationship between power and knowledge is really very simple. The more knowledge you have, the more valuable that knowledge becomes. This is especially true if others do not also possess that same knowledge. *Knowledge becomes power when it directly impacts on the lives of other people* — that is, when the knowledge you communicate causes another person to behave in response to what s/he believes that you know. As an example, let us suppose that your car needs repairing and your knowledge of auto repair is not enough for you to fix it yourself. If you are like most people, you look for an auto mechanic. You do it because you believe that the mechanic's knowledge of auto mechanics and repairs is at a higher level than yours. You believe that this person will not only see the obvious mechanical defects, but will also be able to listen to the "ticking and pinging" sounds that your car makes, give an accurate diagnosis of the problem, and correctly repair your car. Once you recognize and acknowledge your level of ignorance and the mechanic's level of knowledge, something very interesting and automatic happens. You assign power to that person! The moment you accept that the mechanic knows more than you do is the moment s/he becomes more powerful than you in that environment. If the mechanic has been able to communicate successfully his/her level of expertise about auto repairs to you, you will not only relinquish control of your vehicle, you will also relinquish control of your time and money. That is the power of knowledge.

Sometimes we automatically assign power to other people when we accept an idea or develop a particular mindset around an idea. For example, the knowledge that we believe doctors of medicine have instantly places them in positions of power over us. How many times have you placed so much faith in the knowledge of your doctor that you gave him/her absolute authority over your physical and mental well being? Many people do just that. They assume that the doctor knows more about their bodies than they do. Many people confuse the quality of what the doctor knows with the quantity of what the doctor knows. Because a doctor's perspective is usually only a clinical one, his/her knowledge is often limited to the specifics of the particular medical condition. During office visits to your doctor, your body "talks" to him/her in clinical terms during a physical examination. Most of the time, the purpose of that visit is to provide diagnostic information. However, your body talks to you 24 hours a day. It is constantly giving you all kinds of information. The doctor's job includes helping you to interpret that information. Instead of placing total responsibility for your physical and mental health in the hands of medical men and women, why not credit yourself for knowing how to expedite your own healing process?

Medical doctors do know a great deal, but that knowledge can sometimes upset the balance of power between themselves and their patients.

You are the sum of every thought, idea, and feeling that you have ever experienced. Everything that has ever happened to you has also happened for you. The events that have occurred during your life have not happened for the sake of happening. There has always been a purpose to them. That purpose has been to contribute to your growth. The things that happen to us are lessons that become a part of our personal history. If we do not learn from history, history repeats itself. Therefore, all of your experiences are valid and valuable. What you already know has validity.

What you already know may not have earned you a Ph.D. or international acclaim, but what you know has just as much value. Having a doctorate does not say who you are, it only gives credibility to your experiences in the eyes of the common world. What you already know will not shield you from being unhappy, but it will allow you to fully appreciate happiness. Were it not for the painful experiences in your life, you would not be able to embrace your joys. Without grief, happiness would not be as savored as it is. Think of yourself as a receptacle of knowledge, because knowledge is power, and you are powerful.

4 KEYS TO SELF-EMPOWERMENT

Power is more than the ability to move heavy objects or exert brute force. *Power is the capacity to exercise control.* Whether it is control over others or control over ourselves, all of us have craved some semblance of feeling powerful at some point in our lives. Although we may not understand all of its far-reaching ramifications, we do understand that power is a force to be reckoned with. We also understand that we need to feel empowered. As parents, we need to know that when we tell our children to do something, it will be done — simply because we said "do it." As supervisors in our workplaces we need to be certain that when we give a directive to our subordinates, it will be followed — simply because we have given it. As spouses we need to know that when we express our desires to our mates, those desires will be attended to — simply because we desire them. As recovering addicts (of anything) we need to believe that when we have exorcised our demons, those demons will be gone. Simply because we have expelled them. All of us need to feel powerful and empowered. Still, power remains an equivocal condition to have to come to terms with. In all of its ambiguity, power attracts and averts us. It is both a motivator and a deterrent to how we behave. It is as potent an aphrodisiac as it is a repellent.

In spite of what is commonly believed, power is something that everyone has. Unfortunately, American society nurtures the idea that being genuinely powerful is an exclusively White male position. It does this by systematically defining roles for Black and White males and females. Whether Black or White, a boy child is consumed by society's definition of manhood and masculinity through his exposure to the audio, video, and print media. Many times assurances of his "innate" power and position of dominance come through reinforcing attitudes such as "boys will be boys" or "it's a man's world." Because society rarely gives credence to the notion that females possess the same natural ability to attract, generate, and control power as males, many of its most powerful role models (i.e., C.E.O.s, heads of state, and athletes) are male. Accordingly, it is the hero and not the heroine who saves the day. It is the damsel and not the dude who is always in distress.

Power is generally seen as a uniquely masculine experience that does not blend well with the long-standing definitions of femininity. Although it is true that a powerful car may be called "Betsy," ultimate control of her falls under male domain. Most of the things in American society that have come to symbolize power have become aspects of the male personality. Even when a woman does manage to slip through the cracks in the walls of male dominance, her achievements are often characterized as an abnormality of the true nature of females. Unfortunately, the idea of female subordinance and male dominance is continually perpetuated by both sexes. So, it should not surprise you that many women cannot imagine themselves as powerful people or as functioning successfully in positions of power. For Black American and other "minority" women, imagining power is especially hard because many of them have allowed themselves to become stigmatized by the color of their skin or their cultural heritage.

Even though women of all races and colors have achieved varying levels of greatness, recognition is a long time coming. As a Black woman, it is important for you to believe that there is nothing wrong with being an astronaut, mechanic, physicist, architect, or attorney. There is nothing "abnormal" about being the leader of a company or the head of a country. Genuine power is not the consequence of gender or race. Genuine power is the result of knowledge. Having knowledge will bring you power. When you know your environment, you are powerful while in it. When you know yourself, you are powerful in any environment. You must believe that you already hold the keys that will unlock

6

the doors of success for you. You cannot rely on other people to finish jobs that you start, nor can you expect other people to resolve conflicts that you create. Never underestimate the abilities that you have.

Success at anything not only depends on finding a need and filling it. Success also depends on finding a need and knowing how to fill it well. Empowering yourself is hard work. You must train yourself to work towards capitalizing on your knowledge in a positive way. Positive self-talk and surrounding yourself with nurturing people help to make the transition to self-empowerment a smoother one. There are many techniques for achieving self-empowerment. The four keys listed here focus on tapping into the power that self-knowledge brings.

4 KEYS TO SELF-EMPOWERMENT

Key #1: Give yourself credit for what you already know.

Each person has his/her own style of communicating. That style could be the result of the "socialized learning" that influences how we communicate with one another. For instance, some scientific studies have shown that girls tend to be more verbal and articulate than boys. This scientific evidence has become so interwoven into our social learning that we have allowed those actions directly related to talking to become stereotypes of the female personality. For instance, gossiping is automatically thought of as an exclusively female past time. When men get together to talk it's not called gossiping. It's called "talking shop." It would seem that while little boys are off somewhere "playing doctor" or "playing Army," little girls are going about the business of accumulating and manipulating words. While boys are learning to meet their objectives through physical assertion and brute force, girls are learning to meet theirs through verbal negotiating and eyelash batting.

During your lifetime you will be bombarded with a

tremendous amount of information. None of it should be taken for granted because without it you would not be able to function. A person with a college degree is no more important than the person with a high school diploma. There are many reasons why one person pursues "higher" learning and another person does not. Perhaps one person has more financial resources than the other. Perhaps one person's family responsibilities are greater than the other, and so on. Sometimes, we make the mistake of thinking that only "bookworms" and intellectuals have what it takes to be successful. Nothing could be further from the truth. Not all multimillionaires are college graduates, and not all college graduates are multimillionaires, either. Many innovative inventions such as "Crazy Glue" and "Velcro" were developed from very simple ideas. At some point in every day you have probably had to make simple modifications or come up with solutions to make your day go smoother. You may not be a rocket scientist, but that doesn't mean that what you know has no merit. Not everyone can learn everything, but everyone can learn something. Being able to learn is an accomplishment in itself. Being able to translate what you have learned into terms that other people can benefit from is an even greater accomplishment. So, every time you prepare a meal, drive a car, organize a meeting, tend a garden, or do any of the thousands of things that you do, give yourself credit. You are demonstrating what you know.

Key #2: Learn how to communicate effectively what you know.

When people achieve genuine power it is partly because they are able to master the language of their environment. You must master the language of the land in order to reign supreme there. For example, if the land is banking, you must master the spoken and unspoken language of bankers. That means being able to communicate your knowledge of dollars and cents. That also means being able to communicate a skill at customer relations. If the land is hospital administration, you must master the language of hospital administrators. That means being able to communicate your knowledge of capital budgets and other fiscal concerns. That also means being able to communicate an appreciation for patient rights and employee concerns. If the land is culinary arts, you must master the language of culinary artists. That means communicating your expertise at food preparation. That also means being able to communicate your sensitivity to the nutritional demands and dietary needs of your patrons.

Mastery of language is not limited to spoken words because we don't always use speech to communicate our ideas or intentions. Sometimes, we use nonverbal "signals" to express ourselves. Those nonverbal cues are often meant to alert other people to our level of knowledge. From the adversarial stance to the sheepish grin, "body language" is also an important tool that we use to communicate an array of emotions and ideas to other people. You must be able to speak effectively in the environments in which you find yourself. You must also be able to interpret effectively the body language that is spoken to you. Communication has an enormously powerful influence on the human experience. When communication is negative, it can destroy individuals, families, and even nations. When it is positive, communication can ensure that we reach our highest potential.

Key #3: Refuse to be satisfied with what you already know.

The power of knowledge would be impossible without some form of communication. Communication would be impossible without some form of language. Without language, there would be no way for us effectively to express what we know. Even though the language we speak can be silent or spoken, without words we would be reduced to communicating with grunts and groans. The majority of language that we use to communicate with one another is done through speech. When we speak, we try to create a bridge of mental images that will link us with the person being spoken to. Language is a powerful communications tool. It can influence how we think. It can control what we think. It can dictate how we behave. In their book, *Mystery Dance: On the Evolution of Human Sexuality*, authors Lynn Margolis and Dorian Sagan discuss the effects that language have on how we see things. They contend that:

Indeed some linguists believe that speaking different languages coincides not merely with different words, but with distinct ways of thinking, of ordering and perceiving the world. If true, then language directs our view of time. For example, occasionally we speak of what's "around the corner" or "over the horizon" — seeing our future as a place blocked to vision, but generally the language leads us, as English speakers, to think that our past is behind us.

When someone speaks to us in a language that is relative to what we believe and how we feel, we listen. When two people can "speak the same language" in the figurative as well as literal sense, we have the basis for effective communication. Effective communication is essential to self-empowerment. We can communicate what we know by demonstrating our verbal, intellectual, and manual abilities to other people. Most of the time, speaking allows us to accomplish this. For the communicator (the person speaking), it involves finding a common ground or mutual basis of comparison between him/her and the audience. For the speaker, it is essential that some part of the listener be able to grasp, relate to, or empathize with what is being said. If the person speaking cannot appeal to that aspect of the listener's being, communication between them will suffer.

Key # 4: Be an effective listener.

Contrary to what many people think, listening and hearing are two entirely different things. Effective listeners are able to turn off their egos long enough to focus on what is being said to them. Effective listeners are able to prevent their personalities from interfering with the communication process. This is not any easy thing to do because most of us have been programmed to believe that we must satisfy the needs of our egos first. So, in order to create the impression that we are ready to listen, we must present ourselves in as non threatening and nonjudgmental a posture as possible — even if that means maintaining a "poker face" for the speaker.

When you allow your ego to dictate how you listen by reacting emotionally to what is being said or by allowing your body language to suggest opposition to what is being said, you disrupt the communication process. For example, teenagers often complain that their parents don't listen to them. As a result, teenagers "act out" their need to be heard by doing negative things. What the teenagers are probably saying is that their parents were not able to shed their authoritarian roles long enough to make the teenagers comfortable enough to facilitate positive communication between them. When a "communication gap" exists between generations, sexes, or cultures, it is not only because the words used by one person differs from those used by another.

The gap can exist when neither person is able to create an atmosphere conducive to positive communication between them. *Someone has to be able to listen in order for communication to be successful in a positive way.* If you are the designated listener, your immediate judgment is irrelevant. Your feelings are secondary to those of the person who needs to communicate with you. As a listener, the person speaking to you needs to know that you are capable of accepting what is being said. If not, positive communication between you will not happen. If your ego cannot allow you to listen to criticism without feeling pain, you will only hear the words that hurt. If your ego does not allow you to listen to unpleasant truths about yourself without feeling ashamed, you will only hear the words that frighten you. If your ego will not allow you to listen to opposing opinions without feeling betrayed, you will only hear the words that make you angry.

FAMILY INFLUENCES: TOXIC OR NURTURING?

There is a great deal of truth in the saying "it runs in the family." Usually when we make that statement we are referring to something about a person's general appearance or demeanor. We will sometimes make the observation that a person has "his father's hair," "her grandmother's eyes," or "his mother's smile." In our observation of other people we sometimes disregard the fact that familial influences are not limited to physical appearances. How and what we think of ourselves, how we "carry" ourselves, and how we view others are also aspects of familial influence.

The family is an extremely powerful organization. By its very definition, it is an organization in which its members share a common link. As a matter of fact, the term is frequently used to denote the presence of power within organizations, gangs, groups, and the like. It is also a term that is associated with the feelings of comradery and "kinship" that organized groups seek to promote. The link that exists in families can be anything from an actual "blood relation" to a feeling of compatibility or "sameness" between people. The word "family" implies that a sense of belonging is shared among its members. Even if a person is not a member of a traditional "nuclear family," that same sense of belonging can still be achieved.

Whether we were born into or have adopted our families, we depend on them to make us feel complete and whole. We depend on them to "raise" us, to provide us with a safe haven, and to offer structure and purpose to our lives. Above all, we rely on our families to promote our learning and to teach us. We rely on them to show us how to act, think, and feel. Within our families, ideas and ideals are funneled to us as easily as clothes are handed down from one family member to the next. The learning that occurs within our families is a very natural process. Sometimes, that learning is productive. For instance, we learn how to tie our shoes by ourselves or how to recite where we live or our telephone number correctly. Other times what we learn in our families is destructive, such as learning to express our anger by hitting others or learning to tell a lie in order to avoid an undesirable situation.

The lessons that we learn from our family members depend on a variety of things too numerous to list here. Still, it is safe to say that how our family members behave impacts on us as well as what behaviors our family members demonstrate. What they impart to us can be overt as well as subtle. Our lessons from them can come through gentle guidance or brute force. No matter what form they take, our learning can be caused by the examples presented and experiences provided to us by our family members.

It is no accident that several of our adult fears, biases, and preferences can be traced back to our childhoods. After all, we are most receptive to being taught when we are children. As children, our minds are like empty vessels waiting to be filled with information from our parents, brothers, sisters, and so on. It is as children that we are most susceptible to learning from what we see, hear, and engage in. This is largely because children (up to the age of about 15 years) cannot assimilate abstract concepts. Their understanding of life is limited to images and pictures. Words that do not allow them to visualize ideas are useless to them until they develop the capacity for digesting the *meaning* behind those words. Children often cannot distinguish the difference between mature concepts such as reality and fantasy. They rely on us (as parents and parental figures) to do that for them. They rely on us to lead them by our example. As such, they are constantly on the lookout, watching our every move. The more that we repeat our "patterns" of behavior in their presence, the easier learning becomes for them. For that reason, we cannot underestimate the influence that we have on their lives or the influence that they have over ours, whether that influence is unintentional or deliberate.

Who we are (or have become) as Black women can in part be attributed to how and what our parents presented to us. We are who we are because of what was and was not done to and for us. We are who we are because of those ideals and ideas that we accepted and rejected. Although many times we may be tempted to blame who we have become on our childhood pain, we are *fundamentally responsible* for the adults that we have allowed ourselves to be and for the adult behavior that we endorse, because *we have free will.* Life is little more than a series of choices that we are free to make at every point in our lives. From birth to death we can and do consciously choose. As adults, we aspire not only that our children be the product of the love that we have chosen to express to one another, but that they also be the result of the love that we have for life. If we can truly love ourselves, then we can truly love our children.

Before any of us can share love, we must first be able to view ourselves as worthy of being loved and capable of loving others. That is why how we see ourselves is so important. During your life span, you will touch the lives of many people, not just those of your children. However, how you relate with and to other people (including children) will alert them to your state of mind or "mindset." That mindset should be a positive one.

SELF-SURVEY
HOW MUCH DO I LOVE MYSELF?

1. Being alone for long periods of time is very difficult for me. N

2. If someone is being rude or offensive to me, I usually try to ignore it. y

3. I am very comfortable with my physical appearance. N

4. I devote more time to meeting my own needs rather than the needs of my family and friends. N

5. I enjoy a good debate. N

6. If my husband/boyfriend were upset with me, I would do whatever it took to make things right. N

7. Sometimes my family and friends are inconsiderate of my feelings or overly critical of me, but I accept it because I know that they don't mean to be. F

8. It doesn't bother me when my efforts at work go unnoticed. F

9. I keep up-to-date with the latest fashion trends. F

10. I prefer to be completely honest in all of my relationships, even if it means that someone's feelings may get hurt. F

CHAPTER TWO

Getting and Keeping a Positive Mindset

*The sage can achieve greatness
because he does not act great.*

Anything that is humanly possible is possible for you. If you cannot believe that simple phrase, then nothing that follows it will be of any use to you. The truth of that statement is not dependent upon race or nationality. However, it is directly related to the amount of faith that you have in yourself and your abilities as a human being. The fact that you may be a Black woman is totally irrelevant. You are a human being above all else. If individual ability were based on race, women of color such as Marian Anderson, Rosa Parks, and Alice Walker would not have grown to become the first Black person to perform on the stage of the Metropolitan Opera House, the catalyst for the civil rights movement of the 1950's and 1960's, and a Pulitzer Prize-winning author, respectively.

If you think about it, civilization as we know it today might not exist if it were not for the contributions of Black Americans. After all, it was George Washington Carver who earned the title of "world's greatest agricultural chemist" because of the 285 products that he discovered and extracted from the peanut and the 118 products that he extracted from the sweet potato. It was Jan Ernest Matzeliger who invented the first machine for sewing the soles of shoes to their uppers. It was the genius of Dr. Charles Drew that gave the world "the gift of life" through his invention of blood plasma.

Carver, Matzeliger, and Drew were Black persons who recognized their abilities and allowed that recognition to inspire them to achieve. Many of the products and machinery that we find indispensable today were invented by Black Americans and persons of African descent. The ironing board, lawn mower, egg beater, air conditioning unit, starter generator, thermostat and temperature control system, caps for bottles, electric lamp, printing press, pencil sharpener, fire extinguisher, lawn sprinkler system, folding chair, fountain pen, refrigerated box car, portable X-ray machine, and mop were all invented by Black persons. The patents for their inventions are a matter of public record.

The point of reminding you of the achievements of Black people is to emphasize that you can achieve whatever you believe yourself capable of achieving. You can become whatever you believe yourself capable of and choose to become. Whatever person you ultimately decide to be will come as the result of the choices that you make during your lifetime. Exercise your right to choose, but keep in mind that no one ever achieves greatness or mediocrity without help from others. Politicians don't become elected officials without help from constituents. Actors don't become "stars" without help from their fans. Students don't become graduates without help from their educators. People in general will not reach a healthy level of maturity without help from family members, friends, and their communities.

As a woman of color, you have special needs. Your beauty is not always heralded by this country. Your abilities are not always recognized by your community. Your worth is not always acknowledged by American society. Your needs exist largely because of the limited role that women in general are assigned by this country. Some of its members see Black women as unimportant to the positive development of this country. Others see Black women as unable to function as truly productive members of society. Still others see Black women as unwilling to make viable contributions to their families and communities. To complicate matters more, some of the same people who pass judgment on Black women will not always say what they mean or mean what they say. From this collage of interactions, a Black woman must manage to fulfill her needs as a person. Even under the most ideal situations, the mental and emotional well being of a Black woman is a fragile thing. Total well being rests between a delicate balance of sociological acceptance and cultural harmony.

As a Black woman in America, you are no doubt aware of how difficult a "balancing act" your well being can become. You may not be able to achieve your sense of balance alone. Sometimes, you will need the help of your family, friends, and/or community. If help comes from your family, it can take the form of acceptance, security, mutual sharing, and unconditional love. If it comes from friends, it can take the form of support, understanding, comradery, mutual trust, and respect. If help comes from your community, it can be found through religious solidarity or faith. If it comes as a result of religious faith, it can take the form of hope, promise, and peace of mind. However, the most important place from which help can come for you is from within. There may be resources available for you when you need help, but you must be willing to help yourself. The ability to help yourself comes from the amount of self-respect that you maintain, the level of self-worth that you recognize, and the degree of love that you have for yourself.

8 FOOLPROOF WAYS TO STAY POSITIVE IN NEGATIVE SITUATIONS

As a Black woman, the power that you possess is awesome. That power is enhanced when you are able to work together with other people. It is because of that power and your willingness to share it that you are at your best when times are at their worst. It is because of that power and your desire to enhance it that your finest moment is often in response to another's hour of need. It is because of that power and your ability to understand it that your greatest triumphs are often over yourself.

#1: Love yourself.

Perhaps if love assumed a definitive shape, size, or color, there wouldn't be so many different interpretations of it. The beauty and power of love is in its simplicity. Yet, as simple as love is, it is also as vital to us as air. Even though we frequently give our hearts, bodies, and minds in the name of love, we still find it hard to accept love's simplicity. We miss the point completely. The point being that love simply is. Love defies logic. It resists containment. When we share our love with other people, instead of losing a part of ourselves, those people become a part of us. When we accept it from other people, those people become an extension of us. In turn, we become an extension of other people. Love is the greatest emotional and spiritual connection that one human being can make with another human being. It is also the strongest emotional and spiritual connection that any human being can make with the Creator.

In spite of all that love can do for us, it is not something that can be given to others if we do not first possess it for ourselves. In other words, if you do not truly love yourself, you cannot give true love to another person. It doesn't matter who that other person is. You cannot give true love to your children, spouse, friends, brothers and sisters, or parents unless you have first experienced self-love.

20

Sometimes, we think that we truly love ourselves, but when the parameters of that love are challenged, we are given the opportunity to see just how incomplete our love of self is. When our beliefs are challenged and ultimately overturned, it can be devastating. We discover that self-love is only as strong as our ability to tolerate those things about ourselves that make us uncomfortable. If we allow it, we come to realize that we often function on a spiritual level, which feeds our fears and establishes a fear-based comfort zone from which we operate. From that perspective we come to understand that our responses to other people have been largely the result of how we have been trained by *them* as opposed to how our higher selves would respond.

If every person acted primarily on the basis of self-love, self-knowledge, and self-acceptance, many of the world's problems would disappear. After all, people who love themselves do not have to resort to violent resolutions to problems because they know who they are. People who know themselves do not have to invite confrontations or power struggles because they accept who they are. People who accept themselves do not have to limit their existence to narrow, materialistic parameters because they recognize that anything is possible. If every person acted primarily on the basis of self-love, self-knowledge, and self-acceptance, there would be no need for controllers like greed, fear, and ignorance. Life would then be perfect. Unfortunately, ours is not a perfect world. In this imperfect world, few of its people are at peace with themselves. Not enough people love themselves, few know themselves and fewer still can accept the persons they know themselves to be.

In its purest form, self-love knows no bounds. Love of self applies to every facet of your existence. When you love yourself, you love yourself completely. If you cannot acknowledge who you are, forgive yourself for your mistakes, and release yourself from your negative choices, you do not truly love yourself. When you can love yourself enough to do that, only then can you do that for other people.

#2: *Don't take every confrontation personally.*

For as long as there have been people, there have been confrontations between them. It's natural for people to disagree. After all, no two people will see the same thing in exactly the same way because of the fundamental differences between them. Most of the time, confrontations can lead to growth if those confrontations are approached with a positive frame of mind. It's very unlikely that a person will confront you simply for the sake of confrontation. Usually, there is a "hidden agenda" that motivates a person to confront you in order to meet whatever the real agenda is. A hidden agenda is simply wanting something without coming right out and asking for it.

For instance, let's suppose that you and your husband have been invited to a fancy dinner party given by the big wigs at your job. Although you have accepted the invitation on both your behalf, your husband really doesn't want to go. He secretly feels uncomfortable with and inferior to "executive types." Because your husband's agenda is hidden, he looks for ways to get out of going to the party without actually saying that he doesn't want to go.

Rather than discuss his feelings of discomfort with you, he opts to start an argument with you. Instead of revealing what he believes are his shortcomings, he decides to be critical of you. He criticizes you for working long hours, bringing your work home with you, and putting your work before him. Because his real objective is not going to the party, picking a fight is logical. His strategy is to get you so mad at him that you won't want him to go to the party with you. His objective isn't to be combative with you. Being combative is simply a means to an end. He is motivated by his hidden agenda to avoid dealing with what he believes are inadequacies in him. Although his confrontation with you may revolve around personal issues, it is not a personal attack against you. His real fight is with himself. However, the only way to determine that is by listening very carefully to the content and context of what is being said to you.

If you react defensively to what people say to you, a negative situation will continue to be negative. More than likely, your response to what seems to be a personal attack will be to return the fire. Although this would be counterproductive for you (because of the negative energy that it generates), it might be exactly what other people want. If the person confronting you is operating with a hidden agenda, reacting defensively will divert the focus away from whatever the real issue is. When you treat confrontations that are not personal attacks as though they were, you will be the one who ends up unhappy. Once you give into the unhappiness that you allow other people to create, you set the stage for even more disagreements and confrontations. So, the key to turning what seems to be a negative situation into a positive one is to access the nature of the confrontation before responding to it.

Number 3: Try to put yourself in the other person's place.

Sometimes, a negative situation can be created between two people when neither person is willing to consider the perspective of the other. Empathizing, or putting yourself in the other person's place, can help turn a negative situation into a positive one. This happens because empathy allows us to deepen our understanding of how other people see us. If we can understand and appreciate the impact that we have on others by trying to see ourselves through their eyes, perhaps we can also grow into less self-centered people.

Most of us have been taught by society to place invisible barriers around ourselves. We do this largely because society says that we must find ways to protect ourselves from one another. Unfortunately, when we do that our vantage point becomes one that limits our vision. We cannot see beyond the barriers. If we cannot see beyond our barriers, then we cannot truly respect the points of view of others unless they are the same as ours. That is unrealistic.

In the real world, people don't always see eye to eye. Although a difference of opinion might sound like a bad thing, it really isn't. Differences of opinion often lead to challenges. Were it not for challenges and differences, people would remain stagnant. We need challenges in order to grow. However, growth doesn't come only as a result of being faced with challenges. Challenges must be understood before they can be overcome. When we are challenged by the opinions and opposing views of another person, the most positive position to take is an empathetic one. In negative situations it sometimes becomes necessary for our own personal opinions and perspectives to take a back seat because the larger issue is not always whether we can overpower other people. Sometimes, the larger issue is whether we can "agree to disagree."

#4: Don't persecute a person for not living up to your standards.

One of the things that American society teaches us is to do whatever our egos tell us to do. That's partially why we dress, spend, and speak the way we do. Madison Avenue and the mass media have made it easy for us to embrace the "me first" philosophy. Advertisements tell us which car will make us popular, which fragrance will make us sexy, and which clothes will make us desirable. Guess what? We believe them! Because we do, we have convinced ourselves that we should only accept people who live up to what we (have been convinced to) believe is the standard. We want everyone we make contact with to fit into the neat little packages that we've created for them. If they don't, we criticize them. If they can't, we call them inferior. If they won't,

24

we call them unacceptable. We persecute them for being who they are if who they are does not jive with who we want them to be.

You have to give people credit for having the courage to be themselves. The amount of time, thought, and energy that you put into being who you are is no more valid than what other people put into being themselves. You do not have a monopoly on uniqueness. The amount of potential put into you was also put into everyone else. Your "way" is only one of thousands of possible ways to see things, do things, or have things.

#5: *Listen to your instincts.*

When a deer "knows" to flee or a tiger to pounce, we call that "instinct." We not only acknowledge that some mechanism exists in these creatures that serves as a means of self-preservation for the species, but we also seek to disrupt that mechanism because many of us are predators (and carnivores). Like other animals, humans can "smell" fear and sense danger. When people detect or otherwise know that something exists that is outside of their five senses, we also consider it to be instinctive. Instinct is one of the ways in which the Creator has chosen to empower us. Instinct is basically the unlearned knowledge that we are born with. When we bond or make a spiritual investment into ANYTHING, our instincts (and other psychic gifts) often come into play.

Nowadays, most people don't consider listening to "the voice at the back of the head" or making decisions based on "feelings" to be sane. So, they teach themselves how to override or ignore the instinctive messages that they get. This is unfortunate because instinct exists in humans for the same reason it does in other animals — for protection. The purpose of instinctive knowledge is to give us enough information to take the necessary measures to protect ourselves from harm. It doesn't matter whether the potential for harm is physical, mental, emotional, or spiritual because they are all interdependent parts of the whole. When one is disrupted, the others are as well.

During negative situations your instincts operate at full power. Receiving an instinctive message, then, is a very distinct sensation. It is different from reliving a memory or having a new thought occur. You know when you are experiencing instinct. Sometimes, you may instinctively know to avoid a situation or person altogether. Other times, you may get the instinctive message to run during a heated confrontation. You may even get an instinctive message before a situation escalates from positive to negative. Instinct is not scientific. It is not measurable and it is not something that can be reproduced at will. However, instinctive messages are valid communications. Usually their validity is confirmed every time that we ignore them.

#6: Take responsibility for the part you played in creating the situation.

Take a moment to think back to the last argument that you were in. Do you remember how hard you fought to protect your feelings from being hurt? Do you remember how much energy you put into "saving face"? That's usually what happens when two people battle one another. Each person insists that the other is at fault. So, both people put so much energy into shielding their feelings that neither person assumes any responsibility for creating the situation. In reality, each person is at least 50 percent responsible for what happens during a 2-person exchange. After all, it does take two to tango. Even when the exchange is positive, no single individual can take full credit for it.

It takes a great deal of personal integrity and honesty for a person to behave responsibly. Generally, people today do not seem to possess those attributes, and society does not encourage them to do so. Because they are not encouraged to have them, they don't learn how to obtain them.

26

Consequently, "character" in a person is considered to be a rare find. Although we all have the ability to demonstrate integrity and honesty, such things are usually thought of as idealistic as opposed to realistic. So, taking responsibility and being accountable has taken a back seat to passing the buck and scapegoating.

For instance, let's suppose that you made a lunch date with a friend. You confirmed the date, time, and place the night before with your friend. On the day of the meeting, you received a telephone call from another friend a few hours before you were scheduled to meet your lunch date. You spend what seems like only a few moments on the phone with this person. In actuality, you talked for more than an hour. This unexpected distraction makes you late for your lunch date. Because you still intend to keep your lunch date, you now have two options. Your first option is to apologize for being late and blame your lateness on the telephone call. Your second option is to apologize for being late and admit that you lost track of time. Which option do you choose?

Naturally, you choice will depend on how willing you are to be honest with yourself and your lunch date. Remember, you chose to allow the telephone conversation to continue for as long as it did. No one forced you to stay on the telephone for as long as you did. You could have tactfully told the caller that your time was limited. In choosing not to do that, you indirectly chose to create a potentially negative situation between yourself and your date. Your lateness could compromise your credibility, with that person. Blaming your poor choice (to stay on the tele-phone) on another person will not restore your credibility, either. It may only make your date skeptical about making a date with you in the future.

Of course, this is a hypothetical situation. However, in real life, situations like this happen to us all of the time. When they do, we are given the opportunity to choose. If you cannot learn to make positive choices in situations like this one, you will not know how to make positive choices in situations that are more serious. When we make a choice that can negatively affect our relationships with other people, the opportunity to turn it into something positive is always there. We simply have to choose it. When we can do that, our negative choices become lessons for us. Once learned, those lessons become the building blocks of personal integrity and character.

#7: Let go of your pain.

The positive things that we enjoy are meant to be shared with other people. In doing so, they fortify us and those with whom they are shared. The painful experiences also have the potential to fortify us and those with whom they are shared. The painful experiences that we pack and carry with us from relationship to relationship are what we call "baggage." We carry baggage to our levels of consciousness when we don't understand that the hurtful things that happened to us were meant to be fully experienced, acknowledged for what they were, then released. When we don't understand that, we don't unpack our baggage. Eventually our baggage weighs us down. Once that happens, we bring further damage to ourselves and to those who have caused or who have inflicted the pain.

Our socialization teaches us that it is too hard to release our pain; that our pain belongs to us. To a degree, we are taught that we "earn" our pain when we ignore the demands of our egos. What our egos often tell us is that we should not release our pain because if we do, we will lose an integral part of who we are. From that perspective, we believe that we are entitled to our feelings, even the bad ones. We not only believe that even our most terrible feelings belong to us, but that we must hold on to them. So, we "hold grudges." A grudge is a peculiar type of baggage to carry. It is the exclusive property of the bearer. It is also to

28

the bearer that the greatest damage is done. Holding a grudge not only means that you have not forgiven another person. It also means that you have not forgiven yourself.

Aside from being a waste of time, holding a grudge brings negative energy to what might otherwise be a positive situation. When positive energy flows between two people who are friends, lovers, or confidants, betrayal can be traumatic. It is only natural to be hurt by it. Only the people to whom we reveal the most fragile parts of ourselves can hurt us the most. That is because we assign the power to devastate us to the people we care for the most. It is a risk that we take. It is a choice that we make. Unfortunately, not everyone can be trusted with the sacredness of our feelings. When we are let down, a grudge can sometimes seem to be the only weapon of defense. We use it to regain a sense of power over other people. We also use it to empower ourselves. Rather than say how badly we've been hurt, we move on, taking our hurt feelings with us.

Emotional wounds are not at all like physical ones. In many ways the hurt from them seems a thousand times more painful. When the heart aches, we lose the will to thrive. When the soul is pierced, we lose faith in the compassion of others. When the spirit is broken, we lose a little piece of ourselves. When these things happen, we require a special kind of medicine in order to heal. Although drowning our sorrows may seem medicinal, the best medicine is love. Love heals. Where there is love, all things are possible.

#8: Believe in yourself.

Like any relationship, the one that you have with yourself needs to be positive in order for you to grow. It is just as important for you to establish a comfortable rapport with yourself as it is for you to establish a comfortable rapport with other people. It is just as necessary for you to be tolerant and accepting of your own faults and frailties as it is for you to be tolerant and accepting of the faults and frailties of other people. It is just as meaningful for you to be able to forgive yourself for making mistakes as it is for you to be able to forgive other people for making theirs. It is just as relative for you to know what you can do in a given situation as it is for you to know what someone else can do. It is just as consequential for you to have faith in your own abilities as it is for you to place faith in the abilities of other people. It is just as vital for you to love yourself as it is for you to be able to give love to others.

LIFE STRATEGIES FOR
SELF-EMPOWERMENT

So the rule of (military) operations is
not to count on opponents not coming,
but [to] rely on having ways to deal with them;
not to count on opponents not attacking,
but [to] rely on having what cannot be attacked.

To date, there are few "self-help" books devoted specifically to the special needs of Black women. There are scores of "how-to" manuals that address the needs of the general populace, but such literature does not discuss ways in which you as a Black woman can learn to help yourself and develop ways of achieving your goals. The concept of self-help is not new. Books devoted to the topic have gained increasing popularity because of the interest that a number of people have with self-improvement and various forms of "spiritual healing."

Self-help publications are based on the theories of "self-actualization." Both the term and the theories attached to it were introduced by the humanist clinical psychologist Dr. Abraham Maslow in the 1950's and 1960's. Dr. Maslow not only defined self-actualization, but also conducted clinical studies with individuals whom he felt met his definition. His definition of a self-actualized person is *one who makes full and complete use of his/her talents*. In short, a self-actualized person strives to be the best human being that s/he can be. Dr. Maslow was searching for common "traits" (i.e., distinguishing qualities or features of an individual's character) among those individuals. Something that would make him/her more "identifiable" to the rest of us.

From his studies, Dr. Maslow was able to list specific traits that he believed to be characteristic of the self-actualizing personality. Very simply put, his theory of self-actualization revolved around the hypothesis that being the best possible person could only happen *after* specific fundamental human needs were met. According to Dr. Maslow, those needs exist in everyone and occur in the form of a "hierarchy" or series of steps. Those needs, in order of progression, are: physiological needs, safety needs, the need to belong, self-esteem needs, and self-actualization. Dr. Maslow did not believe that it was possible to skip a step or to work backwards along this hierarchy. In other words, the need to feel safe could not be met until the physiological needs (like hunger and thirst) were met. Self-esteem needs would not be met before the need to belong had been satisfied.

The authors of today's self-help manuals not only take bits and pieces of Dr. Maslow's theories and apply them to given situations, but also assume the same humanist posture. That is, they emphasize the uniqueness of the individual, personal potential, the individual's self-concept, and the maximization of human potential. Those features are the basis for humanist theory. Contrary to what you might think, self-actualization is not something reserved only for White people. As a Black woman, uniqueness and human potential are qualities that you also possess. If the theory of self-actualization is true, it implies that people are not born self-actualized. *Self-actualization is a process that everyone has the potential to experience.* Most importantly, it is not a process that occurs on the basis of race or economic standing.

Black women who successfully break the cycle of pain in their lives do so when they understand the part they played in creating the cycle. That's what empowerment is, acknowledging your power. In order to empower yourself, you must step up to the plate and proclaim (or reclaim) the power that is rightfully yours. Unfortunately, such a declaration comes to some Black women after the cycle has been perpetuated. Some Black women have been encouraged to believe that their personal growth is dependent upon their ability to bear a disproportionate amount of emotional and/or physical pain. Nothing could be further from the truth. There is no reason why a Black woman must suffer or maintain a victim mentality in order to discover what her greatest potential is. Whether or not she allows herself to become a beast of burden is her choice, but it is not a choice that is necessary for self-actualization, self-discovery or empowerment. Black women who adopt the "no pain, no gain" philosophy about their roles in life often end up making unnecessary and unhealthy lifestyle choices. Submitting to unhappiness and enduring unpleasantness is not a valid prerequisite for spiritual growth, either. Because we are all spiritual beings encased in a physical form, our growth (at varying rates) is ensured as long as our life force is present. The spirituality of a Black woman is in no way connected to her tolerance for spiritual disharmony.

By clinical definition, self-actualization is a systematic, painstaking, and lonely process. It is a process that few people (regardless of race) ever complete. Achieving true self-actualization in this sense requires complete fulfillment of every aspect of one's nature and potential. In the practical sense, self-actualization refers to the conscious efforts that a person makes to meet what is seen as his/her potential.

More than anything else, self-actualization requires that a *realistic* outlook and approach to life be maintained. As a Black woman, reality can be your greatest weapon against the ignorance of others. Realistically speaking, many Black communities are plagued by chaos and violence. However, this does not mean that those same communities are without Black women who have the potential to achieve self-actualization. Several of the great Black women who have changed America did not come from "privileged" upbringings.

For instance, Althea Gibson did not let her "underprivileged" upbringing stop her from becoming the first Black woman to play tennis at the U.S. Open in 1950 and the first Black American to play tennis in Wimbledon, England, in 1951. As a child, (Dr.) Gloria Dean Randle Scott was not allowed to use the public libraries in her hometown of Houston, Texas. That fact did not lessen her desire to learn or prevent her from going on to earn three college degrees. Meeting her hierarchy of needs included earning an appointment as president of Bennett College in Greensboro, North Carolina. At the tender age of thirty, Dr. Alexa Canady became the first Black neurosurgeon in the United States in spite of the overt racism that she experienced during her childhood. Women like Gibson, Scott, and Canady are but a few examples of diligent and focused Black women with the pit bull tenacity to take hold of a goal and not let go until that goal has been met. They are the unsung heros of the Black experience. Women such as these are our most valuable resources. There is nothing stopping you from joining their ranks.

WANTING WHAT YOU NEED AND NEEDING WHAT YOU WANT

The sage does not hoard —
the more he does for others,
the more he has for himself;
The more he gives to others,
the more his own bounty increases.

According to Maslow's hierarchy, your first order of business is to ensure that your basic physiological needs for rest and nourishment are met. Getting enough food and rest is primarily your responsibility. If you live on a "fixed" income, there may be no guarantee that you will always have "three square meals" a day or live in other than a modest home. However, even under those circumstances your physiological needs can be met. Your physiological needs

34

are in jeopardy when sustenance and housing are
able to you.

Meeting your physiological needs may be diffic
it is something that you will have to ensure for yc
Depending on your circumstances, it can be partici   _y
difficult if you are trying to manage a household alone. You
may be like many Black women who are without the "safety net" that the traditional nuclear family provides. In
today's society, not all children are reared in two-parent
families. If that is a part of your personal history or present
situation, then you have (had) no choice but to fulfill your
physiological needs in spite of the void created by the
absent parent or spouse. Once you have established the
methods by which your physiological needs will be met
and ultimately meet them, you can proceed to focus your
attentions on the fulfillment of your next level of needs in
the hierarchy.

PROTECTING YOUR RIGHT TO FEEL SAFE

You have the right to feel safe and secure. The need to
feel safe and secure in your home, community, and world
in general is as natural for you as it is for everyone else. You
will need a general feeling of safety and security in order to
function harmoniously in this society. Your safety needs
sprang up from the earliest phase of your life. As a child
you learned to make distinctions between the threat of
physical harm and feelings of personal security. For
instance, a small child who is startled by a sudden loud
noise needs to know that the noise will not be followed by
physical harm to him/her. If the face or voice of a loving
person follows the frightening sound, the child's need (at
that time) to feel safe will have been met. If that same child
is surrounded by darkness or isolation from the person(s)
who represents security to him/her, the need to feel safe
will not have been met. That same need to feel secure continues throughout life, from childhood to adulthood.

As an adult, you are responsible for whether or not your safety needs are met. Clear reasoning is a necessary survival skill to have because it can help you to determine accurately whether or not your person is in jeopardy. Being reasonably certain of whether or not your sense of safety is being threatened may help to prevent you from being paranoid about the intentions of other people. It is very difficult for most of us to place our trust in the hands of strangers. Today, people seem to bring harm to one another for no apparent reason. Even though everyone who you meet or interact with may not be a serial killer or have an "explosive" personality, you will still need to come to terms with a reasonable criteria for allowing people into your inner circle.

Nothing is fool proof, but you can learn to safeguard yourself. However, there are a few common sense things that you can do. For example, you should be aware of the type of neighborhood that you live in, travel through, or frequent. Is it considered by law enforcement persons to be relatively safe or "problematic"? Are its residents "neighborly" or hostile? Is it clean and well lit? Considering neighborhoods is only one step involved in feeling safe. You also need to consider the type of people who you associate with. Again, common sense is an important skill to have. Your personal safety can be threatened by persons who seem to be volatile in nature, easily excited, or generally high strung. Although few people are qualified to diagnose personalities, all of us need to be able to read the "trouble signs" that can spring up during relationships. Being concerned with other people is important, but a final consideration of personal safety involves how you conduct yourself around other people. That includes how you dress, speak, and deliver those "nonverbal cues" that attract other people to you. Remember, you reap what you sow. You can't rely on the perceptions of others to be in sync with your own self-perceptions or announced intentions.

If another person behaves in a way that makes you feel unsafe on any level, then it is up to you to disassociate yourself from that person. If a friend or relative behaves in such a way that causes you to interpret their behavior as reckless, you will need to address that behavior. That might include working with that person to create shared activities that are less careless in nature. Achieving peace of mind is paramount to experiencing the feelings of safety and security that you need. Your feelings of safety are not limited to the sensation of being shielded from physical harm. To fully realize your safety needs you must trust in yourself first and remain confident about your survival skills. Your sense of security does not have to be based on feelings of superiority over others. Your feelings of security can be founded on the knowledge that you can take care of yourself.

FINDING A PLACE TO BELONG

At some point in her life, every Black woman will have to come to terms with the need to belong. Unfortunately for some, the need to belong can be so intense that it can override any desires for autonomy, individualism, or self-respect. There are countless Black communities that are filled with uneducated, unmotivated Black women who have given up the better parts of their being in order to "belong to" someone else. Those women often set goals that revolve more around the satisfaction of someone else's needs than their own. When they do, they evolve into "functionally dependent" women who cannot achieve any goal without feedback and approval from someone else. That someone is usually a man, but it can also be a friend, peer, or coworker. Some Black women willingly accept "possession" as terms of acceptance by other people.

This is not to say that those Black women who do not aspire to become doctors, lawyers, or corporate executives have not fully resolved the need to belong. "Mother Hale"

(Clara McBride Hale) is an excellent example of a Black American hero. She opened the doors of Hale House in 1973 with a single goal in mind: to save the lives of those babies born to drug-addicted mothers. Mother Hale used her abilities to make a positive difference. She clearly demonstrated a belief in the right of all people to be given a fighting chance in this world. Her efforts and accomplishments signal an unselfish devotion to her people and a genuine belief in life. The work of Mother Hale also demonstrates an essential part of the self-actualization process — recognizing what we have an aptitude for and proceeding accordingly to the realization of that potential. As long as you can do that, you will always belong. The closer you can come to recognizing your "purpose" in life, the greater your sense of belonging becomes. The realization of your potential might not require a college degree. Art forms such as parenting and caregiving are not to be dismissed as insignificant. The hundreds of children who have passed through Hale House can attest to that.

Those Black women with an unresolved need to belong can be found doing the same nonproductive and self-destructive things over and over again. They are unwilling and perhaps even unable to assert their independence or put any real effort into anything that might improve the quality of their lives. You have met these Black women before. They willingly invest hundreds of dollars on trendy clothes and hairstyles, but are unwilling to invest time in vocations like becoming computer literate or enhancing their job skills. These women accept verbal, physical, and sexual abuse from their mates, peers, and family members out of fear of being alone. Unless these women open their eyes to the waste and monotony that is occurring, they will condemn themselves as well as their children to a lifetime of ignorance and stagnation.

Some people limit themselves to seeking acceptance into one or two groups. For instance, a single Black woman might choose to limit her social interactions to persons of the same race, marital status, or economic level. It is probably the "sameness" that allows for the sense of belonging that she feels. Being "like" others can nearly guarantee acceptance into a group. Most people are comfortable with that probability. Their inability to cope with the dynamics of being different encourages them to think of sameness as a criteria for belonging.

However, it is not necessary for you to embrace sameness for the sake of sameness. What is the point in trying to be someone else? Certainly, if you admire someone, it is only natural that you pattern your behaviors after your mentor. Admiring the words and deeds of Dr. Martin Luther King, Jr., might compel you to blend some of his philosophies in with your own. If you respect the talents of Gwendolyn Brooks or Maya Angelou, you might incorporate their style of writing in with your own. But, no matter how much value you place on the deeds of your heros, you cannot become those persons. What you can do is honor whoever your mentor happens to be by trying to maintain a standard of individual excellence.

You are unique. In all of the universe there is no one else exactly like you. In a civilized society there must be categories and labels, but such things are not a true reflection of individual needs. As you fulfill your need to belong, do not limit yourself to racial, cultural, or economic parameters. The world is full of too many potentially wonderful experiences for you to do that. As long as you believe in yourself, you will find a suitable place in this world without having to compromise your dignity, ethics, or self-respect in the process.

LETTING YOUR GROWTH HAPPEN

The term "self-esteem" refers to how you feel about yourself, whether or not you like yourself. The media generally chooses to use this term to explain the prevalence of

Black Americans murdering other Black Americans. Some psychologists choose this term to explain why some Black men reject Black women for Anglo Saxon or other "White" women. Some high school teachers choose this term to explain why little Johnny feels the need to bring his father's gun with him to class. The media, the psychologists, and the educators may all be right in their analysis. However, how you feel about yourself is only part of what self-esteem is.

To be more accurate, *self-esteem refers to how you feel about yourself as a result of the feedback that you get from other people.* Whether that feedback is an approving smile, a slap in the face, or a failing grade on an exam, the feeling of self-worth may depend on such influences. For instance, consider the concept of physical beauty. Like all Black women, you are beautiful. Your specific definition of physical beauty is probably fused with the definitions that your family members, folks in your social circle, or your Black male friends maintain. To varying degrees, you rate your level of beauty according to their scales. Aside from your individual style, that ratings scale may influence the way that you dress, your choice of whether or not to use cosmetics, the way that you style your hair, or the body weight that you maintain.

The beauty of Black women is present for all to see. Still, their beauty is not often outwardly acknowledged in America. The mass media is frequently guilty of trying to deny the beauty of Black people. Advertisers on commercial television limit their use of Black actors and models. Many times when a Black person is presented, that presentation is not an accurate reflection of the Black American lifestyle. Still, the question remains that if this society insists that Black people are not beautiful, why does it put so much effort into imitating them?

They say that imitation is the highest form of flattery. If you look around you, you'll see that the beautiful features of Black people are imitated in many ways by non-Black people. The White models who choose to have silicon injected into their lips to make them fuller and more appealing are imitating a Black feature. In order to enhance their looks, they must resort to surgical and artificial means to obtain features that Black people have been blessed with. Other women not of color have been known to "pad" their buttocks to imitate the roundness and fullness that most Black women are born with. The buttocks are considered by many to be a highly erotic physical feature. It is a feature that is rarely absent from a Black person's physique. Those persons who supposedly represent "glamour" frequently try to imitate Black features.

Perhaps the greatest irony of all revolves about skin color. Many of the very same people who deny, abuse, and violate the rights of people of color actively look for ways to imitate their beautiful skin tone. They can find no redeeming value in a bronze tone on a Black person. Yet, if that same skin tone becomes a part of their physical features, it is considered to be a sign of good health and beauty. There are people not of color who want color so badly that they are willing to "worship" the sun, paint their skin, or ingest chemicals to obtain it. These people are not deterred by the fact that such practices are medically unsound and potentially life-threatening. They know that Black is beautiful, and they crave that beauty for themselves. This country may outwardly deny any appreciation for the beauty of its Black members, but the things they do clearly suggest otherwise. As a Black person, you don't have to inject chemicals into your lips, contort your body in order to be photographed, or wear fake buttocks in order to attract another person to you. You don't have to fake beauty. You are naturally and genuinely beautiful. You were born beautiful and will remain beautiful throughout your lifetime. Your sense of beauty and worth comes partly from the amount of love that you have for yourself and partly

41

from the feedback that you get from other people. If you do not love yourself, it can become easy for other people to negatively influence your sense of worth.

We are not always immune to the influences of others, especially as children. If as children we were told that we were inadequate and if that opinion was sufficiently reinforced throughout our lives, then we would run the risk of actually becoming inadequate adults. If a Black female child is told either directly or indirectly that her role in American society is limited and subservient, her adulthood is likely to manifest those beliefs. If those messages are sent to her via a mother who behaves in a limited and subservient manner, she will most likely become like her mother. Unless that child receives positive, reinforced messages that contradict the negative ones, she will most likely develop into a Black woman who is unable to love herself. The level of self-love and self-esteem that an adult has is often a reflection of childhood experiences.

A Black woman with positive childhood experiences still needs to have a sense of personal identity and autonomy strong enough to ward off the negative messages that are sent in American society. Your self-esteem will remain intact as long as you remain aware of the source of the feedback that you accept from others. Your level of self-esteem is far too valuable to be placed in the hands of people who may be intimidated by the amount of control that you have over your life or the self-confidence that you display. As a Black woman of conviction, insist on getting *everything* that you deserve as a person. Aim high, because you deserve the best of everything.

SELF-SURVEY #2
AM I MY OWN WOMAN?

1. I do what I have to do because of my circumstances. +

2. No one can hurt me unless I give them consent. T

3. I am the person I am today because of the choices I made yesterday. T

4. I work harder at understanding other people than I do at helping other people to understand me. T

5. I always keep the promises that I make to myself. F

6. I believe that borrowing strength from other people creates weakness in me. T

7. I will accept help that's offered to me even if I don't need it. F

8. Nothing is more important to me than the approval of my family and close friends. F

9. The neighborhood that I live in, the car that I drive, and the people I associate with socially are all proof of my success as a person. F

10. In my opinion, working is only a means to an end. F

CHAPTER THREE

Unleashing the Power of Your Mind

He who is skilled at traveling
leaves neither tracks nor traces.
He who is skilled at speaking
is flawless in his delivery.
He who is skilled in computation
uses neither tallies nor counters.
He who is skilled at closing things tightly
has neither lock nor key,
but what he closes cannot be opened.
He who is good at binding
has neither cord nor string,
but what he binds cannot be untied.

Recognizing a Black woman in the midst of self-discovery and growth is easy. She will be the straightforward, goal-oriented, driven person who refused to accept the "status quo." The accomplishments of Black women who fit this description have become a permanent part of Black history. The refusal to accept "business as usual" could have been one of the driving forces behind Charlayne Hunter-Gault's choice to be one of only two Black students to attend the (then segregated) University of Georgia in 1961. She insisted on her right to a quality education. She was willing to risk her life for something that so many Black Americans take for granted. Many people would question what motivates certain Black women (and not others) to relentlessly pursue their dreams. What was it that compelled Leontyne Price to pursue a career in the White world of opera? There were no doubt other more "typical" areas of entertainment for her to consider. Had she done that, she might not have achieved the distinction of performing at the Metropolitan Opera House in 1961, or earned world wide status as *prima donna assoluta*, along with 18 Grammy Awards. Black women like Hunter-Gault and Price allow the process of growth and self-discovery to happen. That process allowed them to pursue avenues that were previously unopened to Black women, to believe in possibilities, and to engage in the tireless pursuit of their dreams. In order to understand that process better, you must be willing to walk on the path towards mental, physical, and spiritual growth.

4 KEYS TO SUCCESS

Growth and self-discovery are not things that happen in a day. It is an ongoing process that cannot happen unless you allow it to. Submitting to this process will often mean that you may not "see" things the way that most people do. So, your perceptions of concepts like acceptance, justice, creativity, and privacy may differ sharply from those of "ordinary" people. One reason for that may be because growth cannot happen without change, and most people are afraid of change. They can't handle it. However, change is a necessary component of growth. By virtue of your willingness to accept change (with all of its ramifications), you are already one step closer to success.

Key #1: Focus on reality.

According to Maslow, one of the characteristics of self-actualizing persons is their ability to look at people and events realistically. It is also one of the keys vital to your growth. Staying focused on what is real as opposed to what is not real can be very hard work. As Westerners, we are expected to maintain a linear perspective of life. We are expected to live our lives in accordance with basic tenets that mandate that all of our functions be mechanical and absolute. This narrow frame of reference from which we are expected to operate means that we should only accept as genuine those experiences that can be accounted for by our biological and physical "laws" of nature. Consequently, we are expected to accept *as truth* that those entities that cannot be seen have no form; those things that cannot be tabulated have no worth; those events that cannot be explained have no substance, those circumstances that cannot be repeated have no validity; and those phenomena that cannot be controlled have no value. We call this thinking; "reality."

Reality is an important concept for us to master. The more concrete and identifiable its parameters, the more we like it. For example, let's suppose that a man entered your home and claimed to hear music playing. Unless you are in agreement that music is indeed being played, you are likely to question his "attachment to reality." For you, the validity of his experience rests on your ability to experience it, too. In another example, let's suppose that you are talking with a woman who has had her right leg amputated. In spite of this reality, she claims that the big toe on her right foot is tingling. This very common phenomenon is known clinically as a "phantom limb." However, since your reality differs from hers (unless you are also an amputee), you question the realism of her experience no matter how descriptive she is about her sensations. Your reality dictates that because the limb has been taken away from her, it should not exist to her.

If people were merely a collaboration of sensory receptors, there might be a more universal interpretation of reality. Fortunately, this is not the case. There is a side to each of us that often defies explanation, but is nonetheless relevant. The relevance of what is real lies in whether or not it is counterproductive to your positive mental and spiritual flow. Promoting realism in your life will mean not only recognizing that, but also eliminating the negative influences that counterproductivity brings. Such things as guilt, shame, and self-doubt are very real, but they are also counterproductive because the energy that it takes to sustain them is negative. Consequently, they interfere with your ability to reach your highest potential and achieve your greatest good. Although it may seem so, focusing on reality is not an "ego-centered" choice to make. It is quite the opposite. If your focus on reality is true, the "reality checks" that you make can be done without being too preoccupied with self-evaluations. You can focus your energies on resolving problems and meeting goals.

Key #2: Accept people for who they are.

As you continue to grow, you will come to understand and appreciate the concept of "absolute acceptance." This is perhaps one of the most difficult keys to master because you will not be able to accept other people for who they are if you have not first accepted yourself. In spite of how many times we recognize it, how many times we're warned against doing it, or how many times we're hurt because we've done it, we insist on trying to fit other people into the molds that we've created for them. We simply cannot resist trying to make someone over. We go into relationship after relationship believing that we have the right and the power to impose our wills onto other people; to make them into what we want them to be.

When we assume that position, we throw caution, common sense, and conscience to the winds. We completely dismiss the fact that each individual will choose the thing that is least threatening. When we do not accept people for who they are, our vision is distorted. We become blinded by the non confrontational postures that people often choose to assume during battle. When we refuse to see people as they really are and accept what we see, we invest our whole selves into an illusion that we created, until finally, the inevitable happens. We are faced with the truth that not being asserted against does not mean that we are not seen (by them) as the enemy or that we have not been at war with one another.

Your capacity for absolute acceptance will grow as you learn to do three things. First, recognize people for what they are. Don't focus on what you want them to be unless they want it, too. If that is the case, help them achieve their goals if you can. Second, work towards being sensitive to the true intentions of other people. A person who chooses not to live up to your expectations is not necessarily making a personal attack against you. Being "yourself" is a God-given right that all people have. Third, remain objective about what you detect in other people. Objectivity is important to maintain because it not only allows you to accept yourself and others, but it also allows you to remove yourself from situations that you recognize as false.

Key #3: Take time out for yourself.

Often, persons who are in transition from one level of growth to the next find themselves alone. However, being alone is a choice. If you know when you need to be alone, you can be without feeling lonely. As your transitions occur, think of solitude as the time that you are making for yourself. During this time, you can rejuvenate your appreciation of life and of nature. Both are very precious gifts that are frequently taken for granted by most people. This quiet time allows you to confirm that your life has purpose. During your "hiatus" you might experience what Maslow described as:

Limitless horizons opening up to the vision. The feeling of being simultaneously more powerful and also more helpless than one ever was before. The feeling of great ecstacy and wonder and awe. The loss of placing in time and space. Finally, the conviction that something extremely important and valuable has happened.

This time is for you alone. It is then that you will find the inner strength to continue towards your goals.

Key #4: Allow your creative energy to flourish.

Your creativity is a intact today as it was the first day of your life. Creativity is one of your gifts. It is your freshness and originality that appeal most to people. Understand that nothing you have experienced and/or endured can lessen your ability for highly creative expression. The ability to express your thoughts, wishes, and ideas creatively is yours forever. You should not allow time and experiences to tam-

per with it. Allow your levels of creativity to be sponta-
neous. Incorporate them into your daily experiences. As
you continue to grow you will be able to maintain your own
style of creativity as a parent, lover, employee, and friend.
You may not be able to understand fully the dynamics of
your creative ability. Perhaps it is not necessary for you to.
However, what is necessary is that you never allow your
creativity to be stifled.

What the growth and self-discovery process allows you
to strive for is not perfection over other people. It simply
compels you to be the very best person that you can be. The
path that you are taking is one towards reaching your highest human potential and greatest good. Because it is not a
path that everyone chooses, you may find yourself misunderstood quite often. Although you will achieve great
things, your achievements will not come without some
degree of sacrifice. However, no matter how "bumpy" the
ride, the path that you have chosen will be one that is exciting, inspiring, and ultimately fulfilling.

4 THROW-AWAY BEHAVIORS

The human life span can be thought of as one long continuum; a "plane" that begins at birth and continues to
some unknown point in time. As we travel along this continuum, we are constantly faced with situations that
involve crossing the moral and ethical line. Above this line
are all of the positive choices from which to choose. Below
it are all the negative options. Basically, our life spans
revolve around a series of decisions or choices that we are
obliged to make. In order for us to grow and develop as
human beings, decisions like whether to be honest or dishonest, angry or calm, and stingy or charitable have to be
made by us everyday. However, when we make those decisions, we sometimes forget that *it is the responsibility of the
individual to choose and only the individual is responsible
for the choice that is made.* The choices that are made (as

well as their outcomes) help to contribute to our feelings of worth and empowerment. There are some people who seem content with spending their lives crossing back and forth over the lines at random. Others are able to stay well above the lines for long periods of time with only occasional downward crossings. Still others choose to invest their time exclusively in creating negative energy flows with little or no upward crossings.

Different people are motivated by different factors to either go above or below the lines. For example, greed can motivate a basically positive person to do negative things. Guilt can motivate a basically negative person to do something positive. Perhaps one of the strongest and most common motivating factors in the choices that people make is fear. Dr. J. T. Chissell, author of *Pyramids of Power,* defines fear as: " . . . discomfort caused by the perception that something has the potential and/or intent to detract from our life force." The greater the potential and/or threat perceived as harmful to life, the more urgent and intense the desire for avoidance. The mildest form of fear is what we call "anxiety" or "concern," where as the most intense and paralyzing form of fear is "terror." According to Dr. Chissell, fear is an emotion that occurs in all of us. However, we are born with only two fears. They are the fear of falling and the fear of loud noises. The presence of these two fears can be verified in infancy through the testing of our "primitive reflexes." If an infant attempts to "break a fall" with outstretched arms or is startled by a sudden loud noise from an unseen source, it is considered to be a positive sign of normal healthy development. Any other fears that we exhibit are learned ones.

We are taught to fear. In this modern society, nearly all of its people are encouraged to embrace specific levels of agitation and anxiety in specific instances. We are expected to mold our behaviors in accordance with the level of fear that we maintain. For instance, some parents teach their children to fear parental wrath or the advances of strangers. From their teachings, children are expected to learn not to misbehave or talk to people they don't know. Bosses sometimes teach their employees to fear the whim of the corporate hierarchy. In turn, employees are expected to learn "team playing." Spouses sometimes teach one another to fear domestic discord. In turn, they are expected to learn to do whatever it takes to maintain domestic tranquility.

Throw-away behavior #1: Losing control of your fear.

The fears that we have as adults could have been transplanted from our childhoods or adopted from our most recent experiences. For some of us, the process of maturing allows us to expel those fears that interfere with our personal growth as adults. For others, inner strength and courage are never fully developed enough for them to confront their fears. This is not to say that there are no advantages to being afraid. There are instances where being fearful is not only advantageous, but necessary as well. For example, a fear of being struck by a car motivates most of us to look both ways before crossing the street. A fear of being punished or imprisoned motivates some of us to be law-abiding citizens. A fear of transmitting or contracting a venereal disease motivates some of us to be monogamous or even celibate. For the most part, those types of fears that help to protect us from harm are often socially necessary. Not having them could mean losing our ability to function in society.

When we lose control of those fears that are present to benefit us, we limit our ability to exist peacefully with one another. However, not all socialized fears are in place to benefit us. Some fears that we acquire do not serve us and do nothing to enhance our chances of meeting our greatest human potential. Acquiring and losing control of these fears interfere with our positive energy flow and our potential for achieving genuine power.

Throw-away behavior #2: Being intentionally ignorant.

Like other emotions, uncontrolled fear is cyclic. It moves in a circle. The uncontrolled fear cycle is simply an emotional course that repeats itself. When its elements are in orbit, reaction to them ends where it begins. Once the uncontrolled fear cycle has begun, it is a difficult one to break because its components are perpetual. They feed off of one another and quickly become major forces behind the choices we make. "Intentional ignorance" is one of those components. Intentional ignorance refers to a person's refusal to be informed, guided, taught, or enlightened. An intentionally ignorant person is not the same as an ignorant person. The difference between the two is that an ignorant person is someone who lacks knowledge, but is open to receiving it. An intentionally ignorant person is anyone who deliberately chooses to be uninformed. An intentionally ignorant person is one who prefers to maintain a narrow, one-sided point of view. We see examples of intentional ignorance every day. The woman who is afraid to sit next to or touch an HIV-positive person for fear of "catching" AIDS, the parents who forbid their teenage children to talk about sex, the restaurant owner who refuses to serve African American patrons, and the vandals who desecrate headstones in Jewish cemeteries are all intentionally ignorant people. Ironically, what they fear the most is what they have refused to learn about. Their fear of the unknown is self-imposed.

Throw-away behavior #3: Taking flight.

Ignorance (intentional or otherwise) helps to perpetuate the uncontrolled fear cycle. Another element of that cycle is "flight." Flight is a psychological tool that we generate to help us cope with what we don't like about ourselves. We take flight from situations that are too painful for us to face. Our flight can be literal or figurative, actual or imagined, and can be emotional or physical. For example, sometimes when we cannot bear to face what we know is true, we take flight to avoid being in situations that bring that truth out. Truth can be a terrifying reality for many people. So much so that avoiding it seems to be the only way to save face or preserve the level of love that we need other people to have for us. Unfortunately, when we choose fear, we underestimate the power of love. Perhaps when we make that choice, we fully realize how much we need love in our lives. It is the thought of living a loveless existence that terrifies us.

Although it is true that without love we will cease to exist, it is not true that real love is based on what we have, who we know, or how we look. Some of us have been so thoroughly convinced that appearance and wealth inspire love that we fear the unattractive qualities that also make us human. We become afraid that no one could possibly love everything about us or all that we really are. So we struggle to keep those things that we cannot love about ourselves hidden from those people we love and those people we need to feel loved by. We take flight not only when we accept that we are not capable of loving other people completely, but also when we cannot believe that we are deserving of being loved completely and unconditionally.

Throw-away behavior #4: Self-deception.

Like flight, self-deception is another coping mechanism that we generate. When we cannot cope with the potential for experiencing emotional, mental, or even physical pain, we allow this mechanism to take over. Self-deception is like taking flight in that we remove ourselves from a situation. What distinguishes it from flight is that we deny the situation exists. Self-deception and self-esteem often go hand in hand. Basically, when you sincerely love yourself, you hold yourself in high esteem. What you project to other people is what they call high self-esteem. On the other hand, if you cannot truly love who you are, you will project that. Generally, people will then consider you to be a person with low self-esteem. Self-esteem refers to the relationship that you have with yourself. If that relationship is positive, your relationship with other people will be equally as positive. Because we are often our own worst critics, self-evaluation is an important component of self-esteem. It is what we see and accept as truth about ourselves that contributes to our levels of personal power and general feelings of empowerment and self-worth.

THE MIND KILLERS

Those who skillfully move opponents
make formations that opponents are sure to follow,
give what opponents are sure to take.
They move opponents with the prospect of gain,
waiting for them to ambush.

A mind is a terrible thing to waste, but it is a worse thing to lose. All too often we lose ourselves in situations that are self-defeating and nonproductive. We allow our minds to be killed by ideas that serve only to frighten, enrage, and isolate us as human beings. We allow ourselves to give into "mind killers." Mind killers can be defined as the negative internal forces by which we allow ourselves to be driven and ultimately destroyed. Negative emotions like fear and uncontrolled anger are examples of what mind killers are. Like most social influences, mind killers are introduced to us very early in life. It is as children that we begin to develop the capacity for loving or hating, giving or taking, being honest or dishonest, and being trusting or untrusting. In our youth, we are first exposed to the "mechanics" of caring, racial bias, generosity toward others, and so on from our parents and relatives. If they reward us for "fibbing," we learn from them the fundamentals of being a liar. If they reward us for judging other people solely on the basis of race, we learn from them the elements of bigotry. If they reward us for being unwilling to share ourselves and our material possessions with others, we learn from them the basic rules of greed. This is possible because of how we learn as children. That learning process is made up largely of mimicking and parroting. So those persons who are most significant to us during childhood (i.e., parents, brother/sisters, and peers) get first crack at helping to shape our character. Our first exposure to mind killers

56

comes from them. Eventually, our learning is extended out into the community. It is in our homes and communities where we receive our "lessons." It is also there where we are rewarded when we demonstrate where we have learned them. A reward could have been anything from not being corrected when we made fun of another person to being encouraged only to play with children who were "like" us. With every reward came the likelihood that we would do it again. In our innocence, we were unable to reject the influences of mind killers on our lives. So, we probably carried their influence with us from childhood to adulthood

By the time we're all "grown up," we have learned to use mind killers as a part of our individual "coping mechanisms." We're socialized to believe that we need mind killers to relieve the stresses of day-to-day living in a modern society. Unfortunately, as coping mechanisms, mind killers have about the same effectiveness as placing a Band-Aid over a bullet wound. They are quick fixes that seem to relieve our anxieties. In actuality, they do nothing for the real problem. They are temporary solutions to a potentially permanent problem. For instance, if confronted, an employee might lie about having completed an important assignment. That lie may spare him/her the discipline that s/he dreads. However, the larger issue of the employee's ability to be a responsible and trustworthy person remains. In addition to being a limited solution, mind killers require a tremendous amount of negative energy to sustain. The benefits of such an exercise are minimal at best. Worst of all, mind killers can be passed on easily to our children. As a person seeking growth through self-actualization, dealing with mind killers will require two things. First, that you fully understand the influence that mind killers have. Second, that you overcome their influence.

MAKING FEAR DISAPPEAR

Invincibility
is a matter of defense.
Vulnerability
is a matter of attack.

Anything that can be imagined, concocted, dreamed or deduced can become the object of our fears. A person can learn to fear anything that the five senses can detect. Anything that can be seen, heard, smelled, tasted or touched has the potential for terrifying us. A person can also learn to fear those things that are recognizable only through the use of the "sixth sense," such as "hunches," premonitions, "vibes," and other paranormal phenomena. Fear is one of the most powerful mind killers to plague us. Once we learn how to fear and what to be afraid of, we devote much of our adult energies to creating ways to camouflage our fears so that others will not think of us as cowards. When our fears extend themselves beyond those of "things that go bump in the night," we adopt clinical synonyms and idioms like "phobia" and "cold feet" so that others will be more tolerant of our fears. As a mind killer, fear can distort our perceptions of reality and twist our thinking in such a way that we feel completely helpless against it. On the other hand, some of our fears can actually keep us out of dangerous and/or life-threatening situations.

When we given in to our fears, we can become petrified by them. We can literally be "scared to death" by an incident or "scared straight" by an idea. We all have fears. Most of them are kept alive, because we fuel them with our inability or unwillingness to understand where they came from. Many of our adult fears might be traced back to specific childhood experiences. For instance, an adult fear of large bodies of water may have begun with a terrifying childhood experience. Perhaps being thrown into the family pool by an adult and commanded to swim or having witnessed the drowning of a childhood playmate might have ignited the fear.

All too often adults forget how limited a child's reasoning abilities (in some instances) are. Some parents mistakenly assume that a child will instantly "figure out" what to do when faced with a frightening situation. It takes a great deal of commitment and patience to help a child cope with the fear of physical harm. A child must be made to understand that being leery of unfamiliar things is normal. At the same time, that child must be reassured that s/he can learn to overcome his/her fears. A child who is afraid of water can be guided back to the idea of learning how to swim. However, that guidance must be gentle and in keeping with the child's individual coping abilities.

With patience and support from an adult, a child can also come to recognize the difference between being afraid of something and exercising reasonable caution and sound judgment. Using the same example, a child can also be taught to fear water without ever having had an experience with it. If the fears of the parent or parental figure are extreme enough, a child can adopt those same fears vicariously. That is, as a result of the adult's preoccupation with them. An adult who is afraid of water and who consistently reinforces that fear by focusing on its terrible aspects can "train" a child to fear it, too. That same adult can promote fear in the child by avoiding activities that involve water, by discouraging a child's desire to play water sports, and by failing to teach the child to be responsible about water related activities.

As children mature, they learn how to fear other things that can cause physical harm. By adult example, a child can be taught to fear other people who are not like him/her; that is, people who are not also members of his/her race, of the same ethnic background, or whose family maintains the same economic level. Under the guise of racial, religious, and/or ethnic superiority, a child receives adult instruction in how to be racist, sexist, or elitist. For the most part, a child does not recognize that this attitude is a by-product of fear. The focus is more on the child's belief in his/her inherent superiority over others. S/he is not taught to appreciate, understand, and cope with the diversity of people(s) in the world. S/he is rewarded by adults for being repelled by them. Anything from the telling of racist jokes in the child's presence to leaving the child unsupervised to view movies with adult themes helps to reinforce those beliefs. For the child, these things help to perpetuate the notion that his/her race is "better"; that is, the religious beliefs held by his/her family are higher than those held by other people.

A child may use a racial slur in anger against a playmate or another child without even understanding the wrongness of the remark. More often than not, s/he is simply parroting the parental coping strategies observed at home. As an example, let us suppose that James (a White child) becomes angry at his classmate Mike (a Black child) upon learning that Mike scored higher on a test than he. As a means of coping with his perceived failure, James chooses to lash out at Mike and calls him a "nigger." In James' mind, he did nothing wrong. He defends his behavior by recalling that his father used the same word when he talked about a Black coworker who was promoted over him.

The lesson that James has learned from his father is twofold. First, James has learned to keep the amount of love that he has for himself proportional to the level of hate and anger that he can maintain for others. Second, James is not learning that he can love himself for putting forth his best effort. Instead, he has learned that self-love should be conditional. He has learned that he can only love himself when there are others for him to compare himself to and denounce as inferior. In essence, he has learned the basics

60

of how to fear people who are different from him. He has learned the rudimentary concepts of racism. He has learned how to turn his fears inside out, which is all racism is. Racism, segregation, and discrimination are mechanisms that help to reinforce the fears that some people have of other people. When racial slurs, sexist comments, and anti-Semitic remarks are not included a child's list of "bad words," that child can learn how to use words to cope with his own perceived shortcomings.

The human species is endowed with free will. This affords us with the ability to either give in to our fears or to overcome them. Sometimes we are afraid to try a new idea or strive towards a goal because of the fear that we carry of failure. When we believe more in the probability of failure than in the possibility of success, we are destined to fail. That kind of negative thinking creates an atmosphere of self-fulfilling prophecies. Sometimes we are afraid to stand up for our ideals or to be true to ourselves because of the fear that we carry of rejection. We use that fear as the grounds for our decisions not to be truthful when asked direct questions or as the basis for maintaining relation-ships that are no longer positive or productive. The fear of failure often compels people to disregard opportunities that might improve the quality of their lives. The fear of rejec-tion encourages many people to pretend to be something or someone that they are not, even though in the spiritual sense, it is far better to be alone for the right reasons than to be with anyone for the wrong reasons. Unfortunately, many people consider self-truth to be a lofty ideal. People who choose not to face their fears willingly compromise their spiritual well being for the sake of acceptance, personal security, and companionship.

Achieving growth is a far less complicated condition than most people make it out to be. Achieving growth does not mean that you are automatically fearless. What it tends to imply is that you recognize how sophisticated fears can be. It would be a sorry choice to carve an existence out of varying states of terror, but that is exactly what some people choose to do. Many of the fears that we have as adults were probably indiscriminately funneled to us during childhood. Left unresolved, they can in turn be passed on to our children. The fears that prevent you from being the best adult you can be might also do the same to your children. Fortunately, any fear can be defeated. Sometimes, something as simple as a reassuring hug, an empathetic ear, or a supportive environment can help to make fears disappear. However, overcoming any fear will only happen if you want it to happen, believe in yourself, and commit yourself to eliminating its negative influences from your life.

When we inject our fears of failure into the systems of our children, we may be transforming them into inactive, inadequate, and resigned adults. When we impose our fears of rejection onto our children, we may be creating passive, ineffective, and superficial adults. Fear, as we know it, does not exist in the womb. It is something that we must be exposed to after we are born. It is something that we learn to embrace and must work very hard at keeping alive. Our fears can defeat us as long as we believe them to be bigger than we are. Our fears can control us as long as we believe them to be uncontrollable. Our fears can dominate our lives as long as we believe them to be stronger than we are. These are choices that we make. In reality, no person is destined to be a slave to fear. We can change our lives at any given moment.

HAVING WHAT YOU WANT FOR YOURSELF

What causes opponents to come of their own accord
is the prospect of gain.
What discourages opponents from coming
is the prospect of harm.

Sometimes we do not make the life changes that would ultimately be best for us. Sometimes we do not make the choices that would serve as character models for our children. It may not be because we are singularly motivated by our fears, although to some degree fear is a factor. Our inability to live up to the standards that we hope for our children is often due to our choice to be "complacent." If fear could be thought of as having its own residue, then complacency would most certainly be that substance because a complacent attitude has elements of fear throughout it.

A complacent attitude is a choice that some people make because it allows them to remain in the circumstances that they have created for themselves. A complacent person is not a happy person. However, a complacent person is not an entirely unhappy person, either. A complacent person is one who chooses to be stuck somewhere between happiness and misery. It is a position of choice. It is a position that allows pleasure to be extracted from painful situations, hope from hopeless situations, and time from completed relationships. Complacency is often the reason why some people remain in jobs that they hate, loveless marriages, and unfulfilling relationships in general. It is not that they are unaware of the need for change. It is more likely that they are just so "comfortable" with the predictability of their situations. They lack the drive necessary to disrupt their routines. Their fear of failure often prevents them from investing the time, energy, and possible expense that making a change for their betterment might involve. To compound matters, complacency makes people lazy about summoning the self-motivation that it takes to work towards making those changes. A complacent person will fight change even if that change would ultimately mean guaranteed happiness and spiritual growth.

Complacency stifles growth. Complacent people often remain "stuck" in their circumstances until they can't stand it anymore. For example, when the complacency of the partners is the glue that holds a relationship together, each person remains focused on what's "at stake." Although both people may be equally unhappy, neither is willing to sacrifice the predictability that the relationship offers. So, each person remains determined to wait out the other. The problem with a complacent attitude is that it forces you to accept less than what you deserve as a person. It encourages you to function at a spiritually substandard level. It allows you to remain lazy about pursuing your right to happiness. Worst of all, a complacent attitude drains you of your "spark" and zest for living. It takes a tremendous amount of time and negative energy to sustain a fraudulent relationship with anyone. The energy that is invested in self-deceit would be better spent in pursuing self-respect, self-pride, and self-assurance.

It is very possible that a person can become so comfortable with the structure and predictability of a "traditional" relationship that working towards individual happiness is not seen as an option. People with the ability to adapt and change (as well as live with the unchangeable), trust in other people, and balance their dependencies on others, seem to be rare. Somehow, persons without these skills are still able to marry, cohabit, and form business relationships that are maintained for long periods of time. Some people can remain in their relationships even though they have lost respect for their coworkers, fallen out of love with their mates, or have become less receptive to the needs and desires of their professional peers. Somehow, they are motivated to embrace the "safety" that a structured and routine lifestyle offers.

Basically, a coworker, spouse, lover, or any other person who chooses to be complacent is also choosing to be little more than a habitual liar. Such a person would have to develop a skill and preference for lying in order to cope with the fear of change. Because their deceit is often extended to other people, they are able to "go through the motions" of being socially compatible, happily married, professionally responsible, and so on. It is complacency that allows them to engage in such "obligatory" situations as office parties, holiday gatherings and birthday celebrations in order to keep up the facade. It's not that complacent people don't recognize their choices. Complacent people know who they are. A complacent father would probably not instruct his son to "be his own man." A complacent mother would probably not encourage her daughter to follow her dreams or be true to her ideals. Unfortunately, some complacent people allow their children to become a reason to stay unhappily married. They often use their children as an excuse not to separate. What they forget is that children have the uncanny ability to sense parental discontent.

Complacent people know who they are, even if they pretend not to. What's more, other people know it, too, especially the children. Although it is true that children have an amazing ability to adapt and change, it is difficult for that change to be positive when it is marred by the deceit and pretense of parents. For parents and parental figures the questions remain. How can you be the best possible parent if you are not willing to be the best possible person? How can you expect your children to respect the person that you are if you do not respect yourself? How can you expect to teach honesty to a child if you cannot at least be honest with yourself?

CONTROLLING UNCONTROLLED ANGER

To be violent at first
and wind up fearing one's people
is the epitome of ineptitude.

It is a basic rule of human nature that people will only attempt to do those things that they believe are achievable. However, the idea that most people will only do those things that can be "gotten away with" is a partial truth. The complete truth must also include an individual's willingness to take a specific action. For example, let's suppose that John is a student who is taking his final exam at college. From his seat he has a "bird's eye view" of Jane's answer sheet. Jane has proven herself to be one of the brightest students in the class. During testing, Jane does nothing to conceal her answer sheet from John, which presents John with the opportunity to cheat. Because the instructor has not been particularly watchful during the exam, John has concluded that the opportunity to cheat without being caught is an option for him.

Whether or not John gives in to the urge to cheat depends on two things. First is John's belief that he will not be caught and subsequently punished for his actions. Second is John's willingness to be dishonest. Opportunity alone is not enough for a person to take action. A person will make a conscious choice to act based on his own moral or ethical standards.

Opportunities and choices surface in virtually every form of human contact that is made. This includes the social, sexual, familial, and professional situations that occur throughout our lifetimes. In social situations, if the inappropriate remarks of an acquaintance are left unchallenged, that person will continue to be inappropriate until s/he is confronted. A person will behave in an obnoxious way until you decide that enough is enough. Remember in our example that Jane did nothing to prevent John from seeing her answer sheet. Her action (or lack of action) turned the possibility of John cheating into a probability. Since the rule of human nature is almost always applicable, it implies that we are largely responsible for the things that are done to us by other people because we allow those things to be done. When we do not assert ourselves in situations that require assertiveness, we are not only relinquishing our own personal power, but are assigning it to persons who until that moment were totally powerless.

Situations that are contrary to our ideas can make us angry. Anger itself is not a mind killer. Anger is an innate response. That is, it is an emotion that all humans possess at birth. To become angered by the actions of others is a normal, healthy response. The ability to become angry can even be considered a "survival skill," because it frequently prevents others from harming us. However, *uncontrolled anger* is a mind killer because it is erratic. It lacks definite direction. Uncontrolled anger knows no bounds. The instant that we become angered by the actions of others and fail to control that anger is the instant that mind killing occurs. When we allow ourselves to become angry and display that anger in *inappropriate terms,* we give up control of ourselves. When that happens, the person (or persons) who has succeeded in making us lose control of our anger is the person who has succeeded in assuming control over us. Uncontrolled anger is a mind killer that can seem to seize you suddenly and without warning. Like the proverbial headlights that petrify the deer in the road, anger without control can utterly destroy you. It can also "fester" inside of you like some dreaded cancer mocking remission. Uncontrolled anger is an irrational emotion that can test the limits of your self-control and challenge the basic instincts of humans to exist harmoniously with others. That is why it is so important not only to allow your anger to occur, but also to guide it once it does.

Uncontrolled anger can sometimes spring forth from our egos as a testament to how we see ourselves and in response to how we believe that others see us. *No matter how anger occurs, once it does it must be dealt with.* It must be placed in proper perspective and controlled. For example, you might believe that your boss treats you like an "inferior" worker. However, unless you believe yourself to be inferior to others and assign power to them, there will be little that can be done to you to provoke sudden uncontrolled anger from you. Very often we are unable to control our anger because we do not take the time to try to understand the things that happen to us and acknowledge the part that we play in allowing those things to happen. All too often we respond to unpleasant situations by "shooting first" and asking questions later. More often than not, working towards a true understanding of the motivations that lie behind the actions of others can contribute greatly to our ability to control our anger. True understanding is a *learned skill* that requires a conscious effort to focus more on why an event has occurred than solely on what event has occurred.

It can sometimes be comforting to know why an angry word was spoken against you by a friend or coworker. The knowledge that Mary was "not herself" because of personal stresses or problems at home can go a long way in helping you to deal with the impulse to lash out at her. An adult who you may view as "immature" is certainly capable of angering you. This is especially true if you consider yourself to be a mature person. However, your understanding of degrees of maturity must also lend itself to an understanding of degrees of immaturity. You should be able to use that understanding to help you control the anger that the actions of an immature adult provokes. The keys to your success lie in your ability to remain calm and focused as well as the belief that you maintain in your own abilities.

Sometimes when people cannot cope with their perceptions of not being liked, not being respected, not being agreed with, not being taken seriously, or even with not being included in the affairs of others, they lose control of themselves and respond to such "attacks" impulsively. Their uncontrolled anger can be directed towards their offenders or towards themselves. Giving into anger impulsively has several dangerous side effects that can do irreparable damage to professional, personal, and familial relationships. If you do not take the time to calm down and sort through the angry feelings that your employer, coworker, spouse, in-laws, or children promote, you might easily find yourself in an even worse situation. Uncontrolled anger often causes us to say and do things that we really don't mean. It is almost as if we are consumed by some temporary insanity that guides our actions. Even if that was the case, not controlling our wrath is an insanity of choice. In choosing it, we allow ourselves to be swept up in the "heat of the moment." There is no excuse for inflicting emotional or physical pain on to the people we love or who love us. Although you might regret it later, giving in to temper tantrums or maintaining a hot-blooded nature can lead to serious problems in your relationships with others, especially when you misplace or misdirect your angry impulses.

THE POLITICS OF LIVING AND WORKING

So it is that good warriors take their stand
on ground where they cannot lose,
and do not overlook conditions
that make an opponent prone to defeat.

The politics of living can be frustrating, even for a person who is open to the challenges that come with growth. It is not always easy to live, work, and play with others when there are so many rules and regulations to abide by. What is so frustrating is that the "real" rules for social, sexual, and professional harmony are often unspoken and unwritten. In business, for example, we are expected to behave as "team players" even though we may not really understand what team we're on. Because the world of business is notorious for its "hidden agendas," the role of team player may never be adequately defined for us. If you are a member of a corporate family, it will probably be left up to you to discover exactly what team playing means.

Generally in the corporate world, being a team player means that you must be someone who rides the corporate and bureaucratic waves instead of being someone who makes them. It means adhering to the needs of the hierarchies that exist in many corporations and institutions. That means, staying "within the lines" and following a pre-plotted course towards your career goals, not stepping on anyone's toes or going over anyone's head to meet your objectives. Being a team player also means that you never, ever ignore the significance of your immediate supervisors. Although they are primarily just "buffers" between you and "the powers that be," you cannot dismiss their *assigned power* over you. Even in the smallest of small businesses your boss has a boss who has a boss who has a boss. If you are on the bottom rung of the corporate ladder, you will be expected to comply with the wills of all of the bosses simultaneously. If you make the unfortunate mistake of offending any of them, you run the risk of having the entire hierarchy brought down upon you.

The political structures that are present in most institutions and businesses primarily function as a means of preserving order and establishing control over the actions and activities of its members. For Black persons in particular, the bureaucracies and politics that exist in these places can be extremely damaging to their self-esteem because they do not allow for individual or professional autonomy. They also promote a type of competitiveness that is basically negative. One of the primary functions of "bosses" within many organizations is to assimilate individuals into a predetermined group, remove that person's sense of individuality, and encourage that all functions be for the sake of the team. In actuality, when an individual produces for the betterment of the team, the person who will profit most from that productivity is not the individual. Individual achievements are often determined by the bosses to be the result of "team effort." This attitude serves the organization well. It allows the bosses to maintain control over all individuals and ensures that the hierarchy remains intact.

For many of us, the need to belong anywhere is a great one. Some of us desperately need to feel not only that we are a part of something that is positive, but that we are also members of a group that is accepting of us. Corporations and other politically based organizations know this. They call to us by presenting themselves as entities that will accept us and make us acceptable to others. Unfortunately, it is the nature of business to mold individuals into useful, compliant, and loyal participants who can be controlled.

Corporations are business that rely on different "types" of employees in order to survive. For instance, the type of worker who complies is welcomed by most corporations. A compliant worker is a person who does whatever is asked and then some. Such a person would never outwardly question the professional ethics of the bosses. Since this type of worker usually fears the bosses, subordinance is given without an argument. Another worker type favored by businesses is one who is selectively compliant. This worker generally agrees with the structure of the organization. However, if a disagreement does arise, its resolution is handled in as "politically correct" a fashion as possible. This person does not want to appear to be a "door mat," but is also not willing to assume a posture that might be considered "threatening" to the bosses. A worker who appears to be completely oblivious to the office politics usually found in businesses will also do well as an employee. Probably as a means of professional survival, this worker follows the will of the group as long as it does not interfere with the wills of the bosses. This worker never causes "trouble" by voicing "controversial" personal or professional opinions about anything or by being assertive about any issue.

As a Black person, your allegiance to White corporate America is often determined by them on the basis of your ability to demonstrate "loyalty." History has shown us the mindset that White America prefers for Black Americans to have. In the business world, that mindset is sometimes known as "a house Negro" mentality. You may recall that in the days when slavery was more literal, there were basically two types of slaves found on plantations. There were the "house slaves" and the "field slaves." The field slaves were the ones who worked outside of the mansion in the fields. The master of the plantation profited most from the field slaves because they were the ones who tended the crops and maintained the land. They were the labor force of the masters. They were viewed as little more than work animals and consequently treated as such.

On the other hand, the house slave was seen in a slightly different light. It was the job of the house slave (also referred to as house Negro) to make sure that the master was always satisfied and comfortable in his home. That meant that the house slaves had to satisfy whatever the master's needs and desires happened to be. This included, but was not limited to, satisfying his hunger for food and sex, keeping his house and his clothes clean, and caring for his offspring. In terms of subservience, being a house slave was considered by the masters to be somewhat of a "promotion" for a Black person to receive because of the "better" living conditions, food, and the opportunity to "bond" with him. Those slave owners who suspected that their "property" might possess traces of "human" feelings soon realized that their slaves could be manipulated (as easily as any other person) into doing certain things. White folks knew then (as they do today) that most Blacks simply want to "belong" and be thought of in the same terms as *any* human being. Although fear was most certainly a factor, in exchange for his/her loyalty, a house slave was led to believe that "acceptance" into the "family" was eminent. So, certain house slaves were recruited to mingle with the field slaves and report their goings-on. Such a house slave would spy on the field slaves and report back things such as who wasn't doing his/her share of the work, any potential conspiracies or uprisings, the theft of food or property, the presence of an "educated" slave, and so on.

As you know, the house Negro is alive and well in the workplace. You will probably meet and possibly work with one or more Black women who assume the house Negro role. She will be very easy for you to recognize. First, her level of responsibility within the organization may actually be minimal. Although she will try to promote herself as "indispensable," her position within the company may be one of the most expendable. Because she may secretly feel that her position with the company is a "lowly" one, she may try to compensate for that by trying to perform every job that needs to be done. Maybe even yours. Occasionally she will try her hand at doing those jobs that are *clearly* outside of her professional scope and level of expertise. Second, she may have a great deal of practical experience, but comparatively speaking, she is considered "uneducated." If that is the case, she may consider herself to be "stupid" and will try to divert attention from that "fact" by being everyone's "right hand." Third, she will take every opportunity to imply that a "special" relationship exists between her and the (White) boss(es). Perhaps she will remark about a personal incident that was shared between them. She may claim to have an "open invitation" to the office(s) of the boss(es). At any rate, she will want everyone to believe that she has an "advantage" over them. If she secretly views herself as powerless, projecting this special association to you and the other coworkers will make her feel powerful.

Fourth, if it is at all possible, she will have White "allies" and they will come from a variety of departments within the organizations. Since as a house Negro she is basically a coward, she will not "befriend" anyone whose Achilles heel is not apparent to her or whose character weaknesses cannot be exploited. She associates *most* with people whose personalities and/or maturity levels are most like hers. She seeks out (and finds) other women who demonstrate stereotypical female behavior. She wants to be able to demonstrate her ability to "relate" to as many different White people as she can and will not hesitate to manipulate those people in order to gain their "approval" of her. If she does have Black "buddies," it will only be because she believes that they *cannot* oppose her, will not threaten her "standing" within the organization, or be able to take over her "turf." Fifth, you will frequently see her whispering, talking "in code," or being in "closed door meetings" with White people (or with people in power). During this time she focuses her energies on gossiping, tattling, and discrediting other Black people as a demonstration of her loyalty to White people. This is an important activity for her to engage in. It is important because her fear of you is nothing compared with her fear of White people. She needs to reinforce the idea of having bonded with White people through the act of "confidence-sharing" with them. This helps to calm her fears of them. Because she is also being manipulated by them, it does not occur to her that the sense of security she feels is false. She chooses to focus on the idea that important White people not only "make" time for her, but are also very interested in what she has to say. She has deduced from this that she must be an important person, too.

This Black woman does not have to "talk White" or "dress White" in order for her self-hatred and low self-esteem to be apparent. The fact that she will not be able to withhold any information that might make the boss (or White people in general) "uncomfortable" or that her sense of loyalty will only be directed towards Whites will be clear indicators of the low opinion that she has of herself. However, this woman will probably not have any real loyalty to anyone. She will backstab, back bite, and brown nose not because it is the only way to exist in that environment, but because she believes that it is the only way that she can exist in it and still feel good about herself. She would betray a thousand Black coworkers rather than risk falling "out of favor" with a single White superior.

These are the choices that she has made. This is the path that she has chosen to take. You may believe that she is just as capable of success as you are. She may well be, but *she* does not believe that. For any number of reasons, she sees herself as an inferior person. As a self-actualizing person who believes in possibilities and individual abilities, you may become her worst enemy. If that becomes the case, *she will try to discredit and destroy you.* Understand that. Understand also that your job is *not* to fight with this woman. She has more than enough battles on her hands. Your job is to conduct yourself with pride and dignity. You may be able to undo some of the negative situations that she has created, but you will not be able to undo all of them. She has devoted far more time than anyone ever should to being self-destructive and negative. Do what you can to correct matters, but do it without stooping to her level. Remember who you are. Remember that you can overcome any obstacle, even house Negroes.

As nonsensical as it may seem, the politics of working with others may not always allow for your growth as an individual. Your ideas on the job (no matter how terrific) may be scrutinized by others before they will be implemented. Your point of view may have to be compatible with the points of view of others before they will be accepted. As a team player, you must be willing to function as part of a unit in spite of your "maverick" business style. Get mad at the system if you must. Politics is a maddening reality of life, but do not lose control of that madness. By acknowledging your madness and your refusal to "take any more," you are not necessarily eliminating yourself from the game. You may simply be reacting to the uncomfortable levels of stress that playing the game creates for you. Perhaps indirectly you are also admitting your inability to fully understand how the game is played.

Remember that you cannot refuse to play the game if you do not thoroughly understand what the game is. For example, the forming of "packs" is a frequent occurrence within institutions. It is also the game of choice for house Negroes. Pack-forming is a game that people who lack integrity, self-confidence, courage, and inner strength need to play. The object of the game is to form a pack with others equally as weak in an attempt to overpower a single individual. The individual members of the pack are weaklings and they know that they are. That is why they can only find strength in numbers. Like wolves, their goal is to overwhelm you with their numbers, particularly if you are considered to be "bigger" (i.e., mature, positive, and self-confident) than they are. Once they have you surrounded, their goal is to frighten you, cause you to doubt yourself, promote negativity, and finally make you lose control of your anger. When you lose control of yourself as you try to cope with the rules of the game, as well as its players, you might ultimately lose the game. When you give in to the pettiness, feuding, gossiping, and "cut-throat mentality that often accompanies many businesses and interpersonal relationships, you give up control of yourself. You lose the game!

When you give up personal control of yourself at work, you run the risk of trying to regain a sense of control at home. If you live alone, "reigning supreme" might only involve rearranging some furniture or completing a pet project. If you live with a spouse and/or children, regaining a sense of control is a lot more complicated. It involves making yourself feel good *without* making others feel bad. If you cannot come to terms with your feelings of self-worth, you might end up disrupting your household. When you lose control of your anger you might be rude, forceful, or even physically abusive to your family. So, if you are angry at your boss, vent your controlled anger at your boss. If you are angry at your secretary, vent your controlled anger at your secretary. If you are angry at a coworker, vent your controlled anger at that coworker. If you are angry at yourself, then come to terms with that anger. Accept your limitations. Acknowledge your errors. Recognize your strengths. Commit yourself to correcting your professional mistakes without punishing your family for them. Deal with your anger and then move on.

A spouse may understand your levels of uncontrolled anger. A child will not. When you come home from a day's work, a child will "read" your face and sense that "something" is wrong. A child will listen to the tone of your voice and hear that something is wrong. A child will watch your body language and see that something is wrong. A child cannot know what that something is. A child cannot be expected to understand the complexities of living in an adult world or why s/he is being punished because of them. All too often families do not equip themselves with the positive coping mechanisms necessary to help all of its members deal with the natural transitions that occur in life. As a result, the children in these families are sometimes victimized by adults who cannot come to terms with the stresses involved in day-to-day living. Even the politics of families can be sources of stress for many adults. The death and bereavement of a beloved family member, births and additions to the clan, as well as the inevitable shifts in familial power structures, are natural occurrences.

Families are not without their own brand of politics. Like corporations, familial politics also includes hierarchies, chains of command, power struggles, and codes of conduct. Like corporations, families rely on their members to be productive, loyal members of the team. As such, the idea of being a team player is once again an important area of focus. As a family member and team player, you are encouraged and expected to adopt a code of conduct that puts the family *first.* Unfortunately, code does not always allow for the individual's code of ethics, values, and personal judgment. Perhaps within your family there is a code that often requires you to "look the other way" when one family member treats another unfairly, a code that forces you to condone the behavior of family members even though that behavior might go against your personal beliefs, a code that sometimes pressures you to remain silent, even when you know that your voice might make a difference in the political bent of your family or turn the tide in what would otherwise be an unfair situation.

The truth of the matter is that parents do not always treat their children with the respect that they deserve. Brothers are not always courteous and thoughtful towards one another. Sisters are not always as sensitive and mindful of one another as perhaps they should be. In-laws do not always abide by the familial boundaries that are set up between husbands and wives, fathers and sons, and mothers and daughters. Instead of honoring grandparents, some unspoken family codes encourage families to discard them and "humor" what other family members might consider to be eccentric. It is a maddening reality that in-laws are sometimes made privy to intimate details of spousal relationships. It is a maddening reality that the keepers and living examples of family history are often excluded from being an instrumental part of the family's future. Get angry, but do not lose control of that anger. Take that anger and redirect it in a positive way. Talk with family members when issues arise that concern you. Funnel that negative energy into channels that can make a positive difference in your life and in the lives of those people who care for you and whom you care for.

5 EASY STEPS FOR REALIZING YOUR DREAMS

Undertake difficult tasks
by approaching what is easy in them.
Do great deeds
by focusing on their minute aspects.

How you see yourself and how you interpret your experiences is vital to your positive growth and self-discovery. Those two things will have a significant impact on how you relate to other people and on how you behave in general. Right not, you may be spending a lot of time trying to figure out other people. It's important to know if people are reacting to who they think you are or if they are responding to who you think you are. For instance, you may believe that you project an "air" of self-confidence. You work hard at being clear about what you can and cannot do. You don't mind attacking a problem alone if you are sure that you can solve it without anyone's help. Some people might interpret your attitude as arrogant, especially if they don't understand how you can be so certain about yourself and your abilities. So, they will either pretend that they do understand you or they will not pretend to understand you and proceed to treat you the way they feel that an arrogant person should be treated. In either case, you can be certain that they will relate to you in a way that makes them most comfortable and most likely to accomplish their personal agendas with you. It is a game. It is a game that exists because of the baseline level of dishonesty at which most people function.

This society is without significant reinforcers for honest communication and has been without them for quite some time. Honesty is no longer the best policy for people in general. It has been replaced by innuendos, half-truths, and downright lying. How many people do you know who

80

would return a lost wallet that was full of cash? How many people do you know who would try to find the owner of a lost piece of jewelry? How many people do you know who are willing to admit their true age? How many people do you know who can talk about their work without creating an impressive-sounding job title for themselves? How many women do you know who won't pretend not to be attracted to a man in order to keep him interested? Today, it is necessary to weed through an array of "defense mechanisms," sophisticated processes of denial, and subconscious motivations before ever reaching the real person underneath. Most people would rather not go through the trouble if it's easier to go along with the pretense.

People in general are so focused on their own limitations that they will try to disguise themselves as a means of protection not only from you, but from themselves as well. It is so much easier for them to be dishonest. As you grow, you will find that it will take a tremendous amount of courage for the average person really to be honest with you. Most people won't feel compelled to "spare" you any bad news or rejection because they are sure that you can take it. You can take it, but expressing anger towards you is not the same as sharing themselves with you. That involves a willingness to be honest. Honesty happens when people are able to confront their failures as well as their achievements. Most people will avoid doing that even if it means avoiding you. These five steps will help prepare you for the growth and self-discovery process. It will also give you the "food for thought" that you will need to understand the hierarchy of needs that exists for many of the people that you will come in contact with as you grow.

Step #1: Accept yourself.

You will hear people tell you time and again that they accept themselves and others for what they are. Unfortunately, people don't always say what they mean or mean what they say. Usually, when they speak of acceptance they mean acceptance of those things that allow them to feel comfortable about themselves. Anything else will be discarded or ignored. If you truly accept yourself, you will not be defensive about your shortcomings or overly impressed with your abilities. If you can truly accept yourself, then you can accept the shortcomings and abilities of other people, too.

No one is perfect. That is the first thing that must be truly accepted. It is human to make mistakes. As your process of self-actualization continues, your mistakes might occur less frequently, but they will occur. Whenever you make one, no matter how large or small, you should recognize your degree of responsibility for that mistake. *The only one responsible for what you do is you.* You are not responsible for the choices, decisions, or actions of other people. As a wife, you are not responsible for the choices that your husband makes. As a parent, you are not responsible for the choices that your children make, although you may be held responsible for the outcome of their choices. As a daughter, you are not responsible for the choices of your parents. All people are free to do as they choose. Sometimes they do what is best for them. Sometimes they do not. If a poor choice is made, the blame goes to them, not you. If a good choice is made, the credit lies with them, not with you. Accepting responsibility for what you do implies that you can accept yourself. Refusing to accept responsibility for what others do implies that you can accept them.

People will often try to shift blame on to others when they are confronted with their own mistakes. It is hard to admit when we are wrong about something. Instead, people create games that help them to avoid facing themselves. For instance, if a company discriminates against Blacks, it may try to fill a vacant position "from within" before accepting a Black applicant from outside. An apartment complex that discriminates may offer housing, but might limit the units available or maintain a policy of segregation. In personal relationships where infidelity is an issue, the guilty spouses will blame each other for their mistakes in judgment. The husband will claim that the wife "wasn't treating him right." The wife will claim that the infidelity "just happened." It would be so much more productive if people would be honest with one another. Imagine how much time people would save if they didn't invest so much of it in trying to be something that they're not.

Step #2: *Spend quality time with yourself.*

We are born alone. For a few brief moments after birth we have no knowledge of others. Then, that moment is violently interrupted by the first human contact that we come to know: a slap on the buttocks. When we die, we die alone. We leave this life as an individual, as singly as when we entered it. The soul that passes on is not attached to anyone else. It takes a solitary journey to its next destination. What a frightening reality! So frightening that somewhere between our having lived and the inevitable confrontation that we all make with death is the need to be with others. The fear of being alone dominates the human life span. The fear of being alone forces us to seek belonging for the generations through which our lives pass.

Autonomy brings freedom. Freedom brings independence. Your sense of autonomy and your need to be independent may cause you to reject tradition for the sake of tradition. It might be close to impossible for you to accept what is done simply because it has always been done that way. The rights that Black Americans gave their lives for were won because they refused to accept the way things were done. We can vote today because our right to vote was fought for. We can attend any college or university in the world because our forefathers fought for our right to be educated. We can live in any community we choose because we have fought for and won the right to own property.

The "status quo" is often an extremely uncomfortable place to be, as it should be because its methods are often ineffective. Being a part of it is sometimes a "necessary evil" for many people, but it is not necessary for you. Once you decide to free yourself from such sociological forces, you might find yourself alone often. If you are in a place whose people endorse ideals that infringe on basic human rights, you will have to sever yourself from them. You will have to remove yourself from their way of thinking. You will have to exclude yourself from their point of view. You will have to establish your own methods of operation.

Freedom is not without its price. It is also not without its rewards. Your reward for freeing yourself from the opinions, biases, and prejudice of others will be peace of mind. The fear of being alone is not an easy one to master. However, it will be much more rewarding for you to be alone for the right reasons than to stay with anyone for the wrong reasons. At every point between having lived and facing death you will have the freedom of choice. Your lifetime will be full of choices. Fight for the freedom to choose if it comes to that. Assert your independence whenever you need to. You can choose to cling to the wills of others. You can choose to ride coat tails. You can sit idly by while your right to be an individual and to live a life that is best for you is denied. Or you can choose not to.

Step #3: Keep your creative juices flowing.

We are all born with creative abilities. As children, our abilities are viewed by adults as "impulses" because we display them with spontaneity and zeal. As long as they are considered as impulses, they are not encouraged because they are raw and untamed. Without encouragement, they become little more than unreinforced aspects of our individual personalities that are slowly diffused into nonexistence by the process of "civilization." Creativity then becomes misunderstood forms of human energy that are

84

eventually destroyed in an attempt to be controlled. The ability to imagine is a gift that each of us is born with. When its spontaneity is tampered with, it can be lost forever. There are many levels of creativity. None of which can be fully explained or predicted by even the greatest of minds. Your level of creativity does not have to extend itself to that of "genius" as it did with Granville T. Woods. Mr. Woods was a Black American who patented over 150 electrical and mechanical inventions. He was singularly responsible for such inventions as the automatic air brake, telephone transmitter, and galvanic battery.

Your level of creativity may not earn you the title of "the greatest in the history of American chemical engineering" as it did for Norman Rillieux. The title was bestowed upon this Black man in recognition of the sugar refinement process that he invented. Your creative genius can be tiny "bursts" of ideas that give rise to a new way of thinking — a new way to solve an old problem or an old solution improved upon. We don't always come up with ideas that work in the beginning, but don't let that stop you. It may take extra time or money and may even involve learning a new skill, but it will be well worth it if your creativity is allowed to flourish without being blocked by the opinions of other people. The opinions of others who lack your vision is a poor reason for giving up your dreams. After all, if Black Americans of vision had submitted to the skepticism of others, we might not have many of the inventions that they were responsible for.

For most people, the ability to be spontaneously creative no longer exists. They have little or no recollection of that sensation and will probably respond with disbelief and surprise each time that you deliver "freshness of thought" to them. Some people will never believe that Black people are capable of inventing machinery, designing architecture, or revolutionizing any concept. Some don't believe that we ever have, even though the proof of our creative abilities is a matter of public record. That is an unfortunate reality that you must accept. However, you must not let the narrow-minded opinions of other people affect your desire and ability to create. Your levels of creativity may be galvanized into several areas of your life or may be focused on just one. Whatever the case, always allow yourself to give into the impulse to create. Creating is one of your gifts.

Step #4: Break away from other people without falling apart.

Detachment is defined as "free from emotional involvement." For a great number of people, complete detachment would be impossible. For some, its very definition suggests betrayal and abandonment. Even if detachment were warranted, there would be some who still could not bring themselves to break away. The longer you attach yourself to something, the harder it will be for you to detach yourself from it. The more "traditional" the attachment, the less likely you are to detach from it. For example, some children will avoid detaching themselves from their families even though they may have approached their "legal age." There are husbands who avoid detaching from their wives and wives who avoid detaching from their husbands, even though they may have "grown apart." A person can be subjected to years of physical and psychological abuse, but still cling to the idea of family unity.

Sometimes when people lose the ability to break away, it is referred to as a "dependency." A person who is a "co-dependent" cannot detach even if it is in his/her best interest to do so. No matter how destructive the relationship is, a co-dependent person cannot imagine functioning outside of or without it. There are daughters who cannot imagine their lives without their abusive parents, wives who cannot imagine their lives without their tyrannical husbands. It may seem unreasonable, perhaps even a little insane, but people create their own "little hells" in which their sense of familiarity makes them comfortable. For some, no matter how terrible their existence is, the thought of starting a new life is twice as terrifying. For them it is the predictability of their lives that sustains them. Knowing what will happen to them, even if it is something terrible, is far better than not knowing at all.

As you grow, you may be able to view detachment as a means of emotional survival. Detachment is not meant to be used as an attempt to escape or deny, but as a conscious and positive attempt to preserve your emotional stability. There will be times when the only thing standing between you and your peace of mind is your willingness to detach yourself from the person(s) or situation that is creating emotional instability. Even though you may elect to detach yourself temporarily, you are not without your own need to belong. If you are a member of a family or a partner in a relationship, be careful not to isolate yourself to the point where you forget that.

Step #5: Do the right thing because it is the right thing to do.

You will find that few people will be able to appreciate the discrimination between the means and the end. One must justify the other. It is that dicrimination that compels some people to do the right thing. Your willingness to compromise the means for the end will probably lead other people to doubt your drive to succeed, your level of ambition, and perhaps even your sanity in general. The means must justify the end. People who consider themselves to be ambitious and driven will not be able to conceive of their survival in this "dog eat dog" world without maintaining a "me first" philosophy. Their code of ethics will differ sharply from yours. They may see no value in doing the right thing unless they can personally profit from it. It is a sad reality, but many people will be willing to betray a confidence or falsify information in the interest of personal or financial gain.

It is not that you have never told a lie or committed a selfish act. You will always remain capable of doing that. It is just that many times refusing to play the game that way is the right thing to do. Hopefully, you realize that you don't have to. As long as you remain confident in your abilities, you won't have to sacrifice your ethics. The closer you come to achieving spiritual growth, the less likely you will be to accept dishonest and self-centeredness into your personal repertoire. Your tendency will be to stay away from those behaviors because they have the potential for creating too many distortions. In your personal and professional life you will need clear guidelines and codes of conduct. Try not to stray from those. Sooner or later you are bound to run into someone who will try to persuade you that you should "look out for yourself." Often that will mean hurting someone else in some way.

As a Black woman, you need to remember that there are already enough people ready and willing to hurt your Black brothers and sisters. They certainly don't need help from you. America is one of the richest countries in the world. Here, there is more food than we will ever eat. There is more technology than we will ever use. There are more earthly pleasures than we will ever deplete. It is simply not necessary for you to step on another Black person (or any other person for that matter) in order to get ahead. There is more than enough of everything in this country for everyone. The problem seems to be the willingness of most people to share the wealth.

Real life has a way of challenging one's sense of ethics. For the most part, people are so overcome by varying levels of greed that something as simple as sharing with others would never occur to them. That fact may make it easier for you to maneuver in and out of situations where greed is a factor. You are not without desires, but the fulfillment of those desires should not be at the expense of another Black person.

SELF-SURVEY

AM I DOING ALL I CAN TO
REALIZE MY POTENTIAL?

1. I put in a full day's work at my job. That's enough for me.

2. I'd like to sign up for night school, but my friends are already upset that I don't spend any time with them.

3. Staff meeting are boring. Most of what's said involves management decisions. That's not my job.

4. I could have gotten myself a computer with the extra money I made working overtime, but I thought that I'd benefit more from a well-deserved vacation.

5. Sometimes I stay late at the office just to plan my schedule for the next day.

6. I've made clothing for my family and close friends, but I'm no fashion designer.

7. I've been thinking about going into business for myself.

8. I hate my job, but it's too late for me to be thinking about making a career change. I'm too old.

9. Why should I stick around for a boring office party? All they do is talk about work.

10. Women don't have a voice at my job. The men get all the breaks.

CHAPTER   FOUR

The Big Picture in Our Life Experiences

Deep knowledge is to be aware of disturbance
before disturbance,
to be aware of destruction before destruction,
to be aware of calamity before calamity.
Strong action is training the body
without being burdened by the body,
exercising the mind without being used by the mind,
working in the world without being affected by the world,
carrying out tasks without being obstructed by tasks.

Time is a continuum. It stretches as far as the mind's eye can see and it stands still for no man. Time has no known beginning and no known end. That fact is unsettling to man. In his narrow-minded ignorance he has sought to control time. To limit it as though it were his domain. To control it as though he were its sovereign. He has devised ways in which mankind should think of time because infinity is inconceivable to him. As such, people have come to believe that time is something that should be measured, managed, and accounted for. For many of us, time is something relative only in terms of how it supplements our experiences. We focus on what we can accomplish in a day, on how may seconds we can take, how many hours we will need, and how many minutes we can spare.

As Americans, we are obsessed with time. We insist that everything within the realm of human experience have a recognizable beginning and end. Lunch should be eaten at 12 noon. A work day should begin at 9 a.m. and end at 5 p.m. We try to manipulate time in the Fall by setting our clocks back and in the Spring by setting them forward. We expect the human life span to develop in conjunction with our time tables. After 18 years of life, a boy child is suddenly a man. After 65 years of living, working, and being productive, we are expected to "retire."

Our scope of time is so narrow that we have difficulty with allowing human events to take as much time as is required for them to unfold. We find it too hard to believe that all things have their own time. Instead, we create "time frames" for human events in the hopes that those events will unfold according to our schedules. We have decided that infancy is generally the first eighteen months of life. We can only hope that infantile behavior will end at that point. We say that adulthood begins when the teen years of life end. We can only hope, though, that adolescence will have ceased when a person has reached age twenty. In our eagerness to categorize the human life span, we have forgotten the fundamental truth that time is a continuum. Infancy *blends* with toddlerhood. Late adulthood merges with old age. *We are the sum of our experiences.* What we were as children is immersed with who we are as adults.

As children, the way that we assimilate complex realities like love, hate, trust, honesty, and respect may seem "primitive." However, those primitive interpretations are not always severed with a specific time frame. They continue just as time continues. As we age, we may devise a more sophisticated interpretation of them, but the roots of our adult feelings lie in our childhood experiences. As adults we modify our childhood interpretations to most closely approximate our individual levels of maturity. This helps us to integrate them continually into the "adult way of thinking." We carry the experiences of our children with us into adulthood. These experiences help to form the basis for the men and women that we ultimately become.

Childhood rage left uncalmed becomes adult rage. Childhood grief left unconsoled becomes adult grief. Childhood pain left untended becomes adult pain. Left unchecked, time can intensify rage. It can magnify grief. It can amplify pain. That is why we must be ever mindful of what we teach our children. Sometimes their lessons in life are delivered through us whether we intend for them to be or not. This is possible because the mind of a child is like a sponge. It tries to absorb everything. It thirsts for information, and children are unrelenting in the quenching of that thirst. They seem to be driven to know and understand their world. They are able to draw conclusions from the tiniest shreds of information that we supply. Consequently, a son can learn about honesty from the dishonesty of his father. He can learn about bravery from cowardly acts. A daughter can learn about love from a hateful mother. She can learn about self-respect from exposure to self-deprecating acts.

4 WAYS TO TELL IF YOU'RE OFF TRACK

If I were possessed of the slightest knowledge,
traveling on the great Way,
my only fear would be to go astray.
The great Way is quite level,
but the people are much enamored with mountain trails.

Sometimes in life we fall off track while on the path towards self-discovery and growth. Many times it is because we have misunderstood the role that other people play in our growth process. Not everyone we meet intends to help us. Not everyone we care for will care for us in kind. For any number of reasons, there will be those people in our life path who seem to want only to overpower, control, and dominate us. If we allow it, they will. The oppression of a person is much easier if the balance of power is unclear or appears to be shifted in the oppressor's favor. That too can only happen if we allow it.

Basically, we are all powerful people. The difficulty often comes in how we interpret our power and the power we believe other people to have. Like any other capacity, personal power is either positive or negative. Positive power is genuine power. Genuine power produces a positive flow of energy around and between you and the other people in your circle. A genuinely powerful person is not afraid or resentful of being challenged by other people or events. A genuinely powerful person accepts that everything has a purpose. Even the words, ideas, and actions of those in opposition have a purpose.

In contrast, negative power is psuedo power. Psuedo power is false power. It produces and perpetuates a negative flow of energy around and between you and other people within your circle. A person who possesses pseudo power is in a constant state of "spiritual chaos" that

93

revolves around varying levels of self-perpetuating fears. Truth is the predominant fear of a pseudo powerful person. The influence that a pseudo powerful person has is more theoretical than actual because the basis of that person's power is vicarious. That is, this person's power comes only through his/her association or relationship with someone else. If you have detoured from your path, take a moment to think about how empowered or powerless you were when you took it. The four ways offered to tell if you're off track all focus on the idea of the pseudo and genuine power that people have.

#1: Mistaking pseudo powerful people for genuinely powerful people.

The energy flow of pseudo powerful people is almost entirely negative. Their approach to life tends to be more temporal than ecclesiastical. As a result, they choose to function on a "spiritually primitive" level. It is not that these people are without values, morals or ethics. They have them. However, theirs are basically unevolved compared to those of genuinely powerful people. The spirituality of pseudo powerful people was halted at its earliest stages of development. They do not allow themselves to reach their fullest possible positive potential. Unfortunately, the sentiment part of pseudo powerful people lies buried beneath their ego-driven personalities.

Psuedo powerful people are not only spiritually retarded, but are emotionally immature as well. Prone to temper tantrums and power thrusting, they can see little value in experiences that do not offer some sort of immediate gratification to them. Their hedonistic approach to life prevents them from recognizing the significance of mutual reciprocity or from appreciating anything that is not tangible. They cannot tolerate pain of any kind or cope with the potential for being uncomfortable. This basic character defect causes them to resort to a multitude of avoidance tactics in order

94

to maintain their comfort levels. If they do find themselves in an uncomfortable situation, their first response will be to save their own hides. Pseudo powerful people are shameless liars who will distort facts, omit truths, and betray confidences if it will restore them to a pain-free state.

Pseudo powerful people are big advocates of instilling fear in other people. They directly associate fear with power and will manipulate as many variables as possible to achieve it. They understand the dynamics of power and control. Consequently, they have excellent communication skills. Even if they are not profoundly literate or articulate, they have a mastery of the language of the land that allows them to communicate their demands on a variety of levels to an assortment of people(s) verbally or nonverbally. They have the ability to project that they possess or have the resources for achieving whatever is equated with success. This means that they will look the part and play the role of a genuinely powerful person.

#2: *Falling under the spell of pseudo powerful people.*

Pseudo powerful people have a keen sense of the emotional states and moods of other people. They are very good at detecting other people's feelings even when those feelings are "hidden." Although pseudo powerful people use their psychic gifts in a negative way, their ability to sense you is an important skill for them to have. It is important for several reasons. First, being attuned to your emotional highs and lows allows them to present themselves as genuinely powerful at a time when your perceptions are distorted. Psuedo powerful people will try to capitalize on the unrest and imbalance that is created when you allow your emotions to override your intellect. In order to meet their objectives with you, they will become the shoulder for you to cry on or the sympathetic, nonjudgmental ear for you to talk to. This allows them to manipulate you without too much resistance.

Second, pseudo powerful people will focus more on your vulnerabilities than on your strengths. It is imperative that they find your Achilles heel. Discovering it will not only provide them with leverage and bargaining power, but will also become the perfect weapon to use against you should you fall out of favor with them. However, it is important to remember that *pseudo powerful people will never attack other people who can defend themselves.* They simply lack the self-esteem and positive energy to engage in any confrontation with anyone who is not subordinate in their eyes. It is unlikely that pseudo powerful people would try to nurture your strengths and talents. Doing so might create feelings of independence in you. That would be contrary to their position. If a pseudo powerful person does seem to show an interest in nurturing you, it is probably because it is seen as an effective way to manipulate you or as an opportunity to take credit for achievements.

Pseudo powerful people devote a great deal of time and energy to keeping their fingers on the pulse of their environment. In the work place, for example, pseudo powerful people MUST know (or believe that they know) everything that goes on in it. From their perspectives, only they can be the dispensers, recipients, and manipulators of information. No fact, secret, or rumor is too large or too small to be disclosed to them. Unfortunately, they will use any means necessary to get that information. Since not even they can be in two places at one time, they rely heavily on those persons who have proven to be loyal to them. They will promote fear-based loyalty from their subordinates. In this case, a subordinate is anyone who has assigned his/her personal power over to them, i.e., "house Negroes." These subordinates serve a dual purpose. First, they function as foot soldiers, gossip gatherers, and informants. Subordinates are the eyes and ears of pseudo powerful people. In this capacity, subordinates will eavesdrop and lurk in the shadows to obtain information. Once obtained, they scurry back to their superiors to make a full report. The second purpose is that subordinates act as "disciples" of whatever "the word" of pseudo powerful people happens to be. They help to reinforce the idea that big brother is watching.

Pseudo powerful people are everywhere. However, being in a position of power does not automatically make a person genuinely powerful. Pseudo powerful people know this. Still, this does not stop them from at least trying to perpetuate their false power. They do it because it would take far more courage than they have to stand up for their convictions. They do it because it would take far more character than they have to act for the benefit of others. They do it because it would take far more energy than they can generate to work towards the greater good. They do it because it would take far more self-love than they can express to give selflessly to other people. Most important, pseudo powerful people do what they do because we allow them to.

#3: *Underestimating your spiritual power.*

Partly because of the persuasive powers of the mass media, many of us are conditioned and programmed to believe that power can only exist when we possess money, prestige, status, and material things. Consequently, we allow our worth as people to revolve around our personal incomes, status in our communities, and the acquisition of things. We allow our perspective of who we are to be dictated by the things we have or don't have. Instead of recognizing the spiritual power and potential that all people have, we sometimes allow superficial things, meaningless relationships, and counterproductive associations to make a statement about how powerful we are. In reality, all of the power that we will ever need already exists inside each of us. Though largely untapped, spiritual power is our greatest power source. It exists in spite of our tendency to ignore, dismiss, or deny its presence.

It is faith in the fundamental truth of our innate greatness that distinguishes genuinely powerful people from pseudo powerful ones. Genuinely powerful people do not limit the sensation of being empowered to the parameters of their intellect. You do not have to think that you're powerful or be convinced by artificial means (such as television commercials) that you're powerful. By acknowledging your spiritual self, you are powerful. If power were simply a consequence of logic or intellect, that power would never remain constant. It would be subject to the changing views and theories of other people. Empowerment would then become something that would have to be proven over and over again according to the criteria of other people. Genuine power does not come from the head. It comes from the heart.

#4: Giving in to negative influences.

To become one with the Divine Intelligence of the Creator and to maintain a spiritual approach to life, it is not necessary to embrace a particular religious denomination or belief. You can still maintain a positive philosophy and practice the spiritual discipline necessary to fully utilize your positive energy. All that is necessary is wisdom and insight. Wise and insightful people understand what the real source of their power is. Perhaps the words of the *Bhagavad Gita* best describes that level of insight:

From anger comes confusion; from confusion comes memory lapses; from broken memory understanding is lost; from loss of understanding, he is ruined. But a man of inner strength whose senses experience objects without attraction and hatred, in self-control, finds serenity. In serenity, all his sorrows dissolve; his reason becomes serene, his understanding is sure. Without discipline, he has no understanding or inner power. Without inner power, he has no peace; and without peace where is the joy?

You are powerful not only because of the spiritual connections that you choose to make. You are powerful whenever you allow yourself to be controlled by your "higher self." It is the higher self that rejects such things as guilt, fear, anger, and self-doubt. It is the higher self who refuses to give in to their negative influences. You are powerful when you devote your energy to pursuing your greatest potential and highest good. Your genuine power radiates from the inside out; not from the outside in, as it does with pseudo powerful people. Stretch yourself beyond your comfort zones, because each experience that you have is a valid and valuable part of your ongoing learning process. To be genuinely powerful, you must believe not only that every thing happens for a purpose, but that ultimately the purpose serves the greater good.

HEARING WHAT TIME IS TELLING YOU

This is an all too familiar scenario: A female in her early teens becomes pregnant. After her initial fear of parental wrath has subsided, she chooses to keep her baby. She wants someone who will love her *unconditionally.* Someone she can be with who won't make unreasonable sexual or emotional demands on her. Someone who won't judge her for not finishing high school or for settling for welfare handouts. The pregnancy is allowed to progress to full term and the teenager gives birth to a bouncing baby boy. He has his father's smile. At least as far as she can remember. The father of the child has not provided any support whatsoever, let alone a smile.

At any rate, mother and child are doing fine. He is a strong, healthy, energetic male child. A good baby in many respects. Not overly anxious about a tardy feeding or neglected diaper changes. Unfortunately, the honeymoon period between this new mom and the infant is cut short by her natural desire to experience the less adult aspects of young adulthood. So, this young mother "gives" her son to her own mother to raise while she goes about the business of being a teenager. Through the eyes of this child, he has been abandoned. The fact that he may be receiving adequate care and mothering from his grandmother is irrelevant. He knows who his "real" mother is. The fact that his grandmother is loving and caring may not be enough for this child. While he responds well to his grandmother's love, it may not replace the love that he needs from his biological mother. It is a tragic reality that this young person must carry the burden of feelings of abandonment and betrayal on his young shoulders. It is too heavy a load for him to manage. Although he may never be able to verbalize it, he may always be haunted by questions of his worth as a person. Deep inside he may ask himself, "Why wasn't I good enough for my mother to keep?"; "What's wrong with me?"; "What did I do wrong?"

In another community, a teenager gives birth to a bright-eyed baby girl who was fathered by a person not even old enough to buy a beer. Delivered to a mother concerned more with getting "high" than with getting proper prenatal care. A mother whose preference for drugs and alcohol eventually proved too fatal a combination. Sadly, this beautiful baby girl soon finds herself alone. Her biological father changes his mind about fatherhood and opts to pass the task of raising his daughter onto the first persons willing to accommodate him. Bundled and bowed, she is given to a nearby aunt and uncle to raise. There, she receives lodging, support, kindness, and the truth about her parentage. This baby girl grows into a young woman who struggles to come to terms with her parents' betrayal. She is especially troubled by the betrayal of her father. As time passes, she grieves. She mourns the death of a mother she never knew and the loss of a father who did not want to know her.

We have no idea how our choices will affect "the big picture" that we call a lifetime. Within our lifetime, our choices have long- and short-term consequences. When the children have children, that truth remains. The babies of our babies may be children who valiantly struggle to come to terms with their feelings of desertion by their mother or father. We have children who must accept the fact that the first people with whom they have identified have discarded them. We have children who must somehow differentiate the boundaries between being a grandchild or niece and being a sibling. We have children who must function as both a secondary relative and a sibling to a surrogate parent. To make matters worse, the biological parents may only make "obligatory" gestures to the children. That is, making only annual appearances for birthdays or holidays. Many will not bother to show up at all.

In the long of it, we may have adults with unresolved childhood emotions and untended pain. We may have adults who must fight to come to terms with love–hate feelings for their biological parents. Society-at-large has ensured that the *ideal* of motherhood or fatherhood has been firmly implanted into the consciousness of our children. That ideal is not lessened by time. They may secretly yearn for the mother-son/father-daughter love that so many of their peers and friends speak about. At the same time, we may have adults who are deeply resentful of their parents' decision to give them away *for any reason.* As adults, they may not be able to understand or fully accept why they were "cheated" out of the full benefits of being a son or daughter to a biological parent.

When most of us think about the ramifications of teenage pregnancy, we focus on the stifling effects that pregnancy can have on the lives our teens. We fret about the lack of parenting skills that our teens have. We sometimes forget that the children of our teenagers eventually grow up. We may not stop to consider that those children will be mainstreamed into a society that says that mothers who love their sons and fathers who love their daughters do not give them away. As adults they will be expected to function just like everyone else. They will be surrounded by people from nuclear families. They will be expected to fit in with everyone else. However, the child of a teenage parent may not be able to forgive the fact that the parent–child relationship or the potential for that relationship was violated.

The babies of babies may grow up to be permanently scarred adults. Imagine a male child growing up to become an adult who constantly searches for his mother in other women. Such a quest may be never ending. He may look for her everywhere and in many different women. He may have several lovers, but in addition to the sexual gratification that he receives, there may be strong maternal ties to these women. Whether it is conscious, subconscious, or unconscious, we may not be above preying upon these women with whom the strongest maternal instincts can be detected. His "harem" may consist of those women who will care for him when he is sick. Women who will calm him when he is afraid. Women who will inspire him when he is discouraged. Women who will feed and clothe him. Women who will see to his earthly needs. Women who will "mother" him.

The baby girl of a teenage mother may also grow up to be an adult who struggles to come to terms with her parents' betrayal. Like her counterpart, she may engage in a relentless search for her absent father. She looks for men who need to be needed. Perhaps even hoping to meet men in search of their "lost" daughters. She may be no stranger to multiple relationships and is perhaps eager to be "fathered" by as many men as possible. She may not be ashamed to admit her preference for "Sugar Daddies," for men several years her senior, or for men who lack the will power to resist her charms. She will do whatever it takes to be taken care of by them.

In a very real sense, the actions of an immature teenager can create a dysfunctional adult. Adults who may not be able to control the urge to "replace" their fathers or mothers because of the void created by their abandonment. Certainly not all children born to adolescent parents grow up to be self-destructive adults, but even if one of them does, it is too many. It is unreasonable to deny that the stages of life are dependent upon one another for healthy completion. Not all emotions will be outgrown. Especially those painful childhood emotions that were left unattended to. As an adult you may be able to recall the sensation of being held as an infant. You may be able to describe many of your childhood experiences in vivid detail. Grammar school incidents, discipline from parents for childhood pranks, budding sexuality, and the death of loved ones are all events that serve to make us complete persons. All of us carry these kinds of memories with us. Our yesterdays help to make up our todays and forecast our tomorrows.

We have a responsibility to our children. We are obligated to all of them whether we are parents or not. If as adults we conduct ourselves and our lives haphazardly, without regard for the signals that we send to our youth, we are nothing more than self-fulfilling prophets. As such, we will teach our children that it is acceptable to be irresponsible. We will teach our children that self-respect is optional. We will be confirming that commitment to family is unnecessary. We will be condoning that strength of character is not a requirement. We will be affirming that lack of discipline is not a deterrent to success. We will be validating that self-love is unimportant.

The children of today are the congressmen, doctors, corporate executives, and social leaders of tomorrow. As adults we have a responsibility to ensure that the legacy for them is left intact. The children of our teenagers are also our responsibility. What they grow up to become is largely a result of our doing. Children from single-parent homes, children with alcohol- and drug-addicted parents, children reared in permissive and unstructured households, as well as children raised by physically and mentally abusive family members, are all children who we can love.

We have an opportunity to teach our children many

things. However, we will not be able to instill positive values into our children if we do not possess them ourselves. As a parent it will be difficult to teach your children to respect the right, property, and privacy of others if you habitually invade theirs. As a mentor you will not be able to exemplify diplomacy if you are consistently unable to resolve disputes amicably. As a mother you will not be able to convince children of the importance of honesty if you are not true to yourself or cannot stand up for your own beliefs. As a father you will not be able to demonstrate inner strength if you are unwilling to stand up and fight for what you (and you children) know is right. In short, before you can begin with your efforts to mold your children, you must make sure that you are an appropriate representative of the ideals that you hope to set forth.

HOLDING YOURSELF ACCOUNTABLE

Once upon a time, in the not too distant past, a wonderful kingdom existed. This kingdom was one of the richest in the world. For its people there was more wealth than could ever be enjoyed in a single lifetime. There was more food than could ever be eaten and more technology than could ever be utilized. Best of all, the children of the kingdom were its most prized citizens. The schools were committed to fulfilling the intellectual, physical, and emotional needs of the children. Communities throughout the land gave freely of their support and encouragement to the children. The homes of the children were places of love and stability. This was a wonderful place to be and a wonderful time to be a child.

One day a great dark cloud fell upon the entire kingdom. It was a cloud so thick and ominous that the elders of the kingdom were blinded. They could not see the beauty of the land. They could not see the value in human life. Worst of all, they could not see the importance of loving the children. As the cloud loomed over head, many of the people in this land of plenty were allowed to die of starvation, live in poverty, embrace ignorance and intolerance, and disregard their children. Sadly, the schools became battlegrounds. Homes became increasingly unstable. Communities everywhere seemed deaf to the pleas of the children for help. In time, the children of the kingdom became embittered because the elders had forsaken them. A terrible war between the children of the kingdom and its elders soon followed. In their anger, the children bore arms against their families, their schools, their communities, and even themselves.

After many years of fighting, the elders began to realize what the children were so angry about. The elders not only began to listen, but also began to *hear* what the children had been trying to say during all the years of fighting. With time, the elders were able to mend all of the fences that were destroyed by their failure to truly love the children. The children forgave the elders and went on to be committed, responsible leaders throughout the land. And they lived happily ever after.

What you have just read is not a fairy tale. It is a simplified illustration of social erosion. The kingdom in the story is America and the fall of America's children is quite real. The story's cloud is a reference to the contemporary forces in society that were created by the elders. The preceding was meant to illustrate the children's response to those contemporary forces that were set in motion by the adults. The tale was given a happy ending because a happy ending is possible.

America is one of the richest "kingdoms" in the world. Americans have more of nearly everything than any other people. Yet, an alarming number of its inhabitants are homeless, malnourished, and illiterate. Even without the existence of full-scale civil, religious, or ethnic wars, Americans have the dubious distinction of being the most violent people in the world. Being a "super power" has not protected Americans from themselves. In our rush to make our lives "better," acquire wealth, secure power, and generally reign supreme, we have sacrificed our children. Our eagerness to bear arms has helped to create child assassins. Our need for escapism has helped to create teenage alcoholics, crack babies, and chemically dependent children. Our insistence on being a purely profit-driven country has helped to create teenage drug lords, kidnappers, and bank robbers. Our willingness to allow the moral fiber of our communities to unravel has helped to create child prostitutes and adolescent parents. Our failure to live up to the ideals that we claim to hold so dear have helped to create the next generation of Klansmen, "skinheads," and an array of underage hatemongers.

When we look at our youth today, we forget (or deny) that our children are nothing more than what we have *allowed* them to become. We, the adults, have paved the way for our children's paths today. The road they travel is partly the result of being denied those things that would have ensured their development *as children*. Children are not just "little people" or smaller versions of ourselves. They cannot be expected to develop as children in the role of "latch key kids" or surrogate homemakers in our absence. Today we are at war with our children largely because we are so out of touch with them *as people.* Today, many of us live in fear of our children. Perhaps we do not fear our own children, but at some point in our adult lives we have had to come to terms with our fear of what someone else's child might do to us. We are afraid of our children because we know that they will not always obey us. We know that some of them will rebel against us. We know that some of them will hate us. We know that some of them will even murder us.

The fear that we have of America's children is like a giant octopus whose tentacles represent all of the things that being afraid perpetuates. We are afraid of our children.

So, when they shout at us, we shout back even louder. When they push, we shove. When they are disrespectful, we in turn seek to humiliate them. When they are forceful, we try to overpower their forcefulness with physical aggression. Very often, adults will "talk at" children and lecture to them about "the good old days" of their youth. It is a ritual that so many adults engage in to shame children into being children. Unfortunately, trying to remind a child of a time that has almost no relevance for him/her is a waste of time. How can today's children be expected to relate to recollections of your childhood? How are children supposed to respond to, "When I was coming up, children were children"; When I was a kid, I never talked back to my parents" When I was a kid, we were happy to be able to play with the toys that we made ourselves."; When I was a kid, I listened when the teacher talked"? Our children can only respond to the realities that adults have created for them today.

Before you try to condemn your child for not being the child that you were, take a moment to consider a few things. If you are a "baby boomer" or older, your schools were probably not dangerously overcrowded. Your high school teacher was probably not faced with having to deal with students suffering from severe behavioral problems, undiagnosed learning deficits, psychologicial disorders, and chemical dependencies during the process of trying to educate you *and* thirty or more other children. When you were in high school, the definition of a "rambunctious child" was probably one who chewed gum in class or spoke out of turn. It was not a child with a semi-automatic weapon trying to "blow away" the teacher because of a failing grade. You probably had the love and support of two parents. Even if your mom did work, she somehow made the time to fulfill her parental responsibilities. Dad was able to make enough money to support the whole family. During your teen years, homes with single parents or working mothers were more the exception than the rule. Parents were able to provide children with the structure, support, and consistent supervision that their growing minds and bodies called for.

Even if you were the product of a single-parent home, your community served as an excellent extended family. Everyone knew everyone in your neighborhood. When one family was in trouble, many of the other families rallied to help. When children came home from school, their parents made sure that their television viewing time was a family activity. They not only monitored what children watched on television, but frequently watched with them. They exercised parental control and knew what their children would be exposed to before the children did. The toys that parents bought for their children were ones that sparked their imaginations. The parents saw to that. Christmastime meant receiving toys that were "kid powered," not high tech. When you were a kid, sports stars didn't lend their names to $80.00 tennis shoes. The pressure of kids to look "cool" probably wasn't as much of an expensive and potentially life-threatening undertaking as it is today. For you, athletic wear was limited to a sturdy pair of tennis shoes and a team jacket that was *earned* through hard work and team effort. They were not obtained at gun point. When you were a kid, the values of your parents vastly differed from the values of parents today. This generation of parents seem to have strayed away from the "no nonsense" approach of their parents. For this generation of adults, somewhere between being a child and raising a child a change has occurred. During that process, many of the mechanisms that existed for you as a child are no longer in place for today's children.

There seems to have been a radical shift in family values and individual priorities over the last thirty years or so. Exactly why that shift occurred is anybody's guess. Perhaps it was during the "turbulent 60's" when the "collective guilt" of the entire country was awakened and the cries for

108

social change could not go unanswered. Maybe it was during America's coming of age in the 70's that made a lot of us feel optimistic about the future and certain about getting our piece of the American Dream. It could have even happened during the "me decade" of the 80's when many of us seemed to accept the notion of "taking care of number one" and reject the idea of being "my brother's keeper." Whenever it happened, however it happened, we were terribly unprepared for the consequences of our choices. We allowed the systematic closing of our children's recreation centers and youth support facilities *without* providing alternative outlets for them. Those types of community centers not only helped to create a sense of comradery among the children, but also provided a vehicle through which their youthful energies could be positively addressed. These were the places when our children could be children. Yet, we act outraged when children congregate on street corners or relieve their boredom through malicious mischief.

At some point in our adult lives, we decided that two incomes were better than one. The economic realities changed for us. A pay check for Mom became equally as important as the one from Dad. So, the surplus of quality time allotted to our children was drastically reduced. We needed someone to act as proxy for us. Consequently, unsupervised television viewing by our children quickly became the surrogate parents that we were looking for. Yet, we are shocked when our children do not aspire to be like us and opt to emulate rock stars or million dollar athletes. We are appalled when our children know more about sex than we do or are not modest about translating their fascination into premarital experiments. We are dumbfounded when our children seem to place more value in superficial encounters than in meaningful relationships with other people. We complain that television does not accurately portray who we are. We grumble that it contains too much sex, too much violence, and too little wholesome entertainment. Still, we plop our children down in front of it and rely on it to fill the void created by our absence. We notice that our children's time is often marred by violent reenactments of television plots and movies, yet we buy toys with "kung fu grips," "slime" compartments, and action poses for them. We acknowledge that our children often lack imagination or are unable to problem solve. Still, we give them toys that are so computerized and mechanized that encouragement for a child to think is almost nonexistent.

The point of all this is not to lecture you about parenting. Parenting is a very challenging job. It is a full-time job. It is assumed that if you are a parent, you take your job seriously. However, as a parent and/or parental figure, you might take a moment to consider the consequences of asking a child with low self-esteem, no real identity, an underdeveloped sense of morality, and limited cognitive skills to fend for him/herself. The possibilities are endless.

THE POWER TO HEAL OURSELVES

Perhaps the greatest asset that you possess that determines your state of being is free will. You have been empowered with the ability to choose. Believe it or not, you have been empowered with that ability to ensure happiness for yourself. You are the only person who can ensure your happiness. When you are hurt by the words or actions of another person, you are the only person who can allow healing to occur. Healing is something that we generally empower other people to do for us. It is not something that we have been socialized to believe that we can do for ourselves. Try convincing the woman next door that she could rid herself of her chronic back pain by changing the way she thinks. Try to get your boss to believe that his migraine headaches just might be caused by the painful childhood memories that he won't let go of. Try getting your spouse to understand that the churning in his stomach might stop if he would learn how to forgive and release other people.

110

Many of us exercise and diet to maintain our physical selves, relieve our physical pain, or prolong our lives. In our quest for overall health we often forget that we are the prime instigators against our mental and spiritual well being.

For most people, healing is something that comes first as a result of what someone else has done to them, and second, as a result of what someone else has told them to do. Or so they believe. How many times have you taken an aspirin for a headache without considering what caused the headache in the first place? How many times have you suffered back pain and attributed it to some external force? When we're ailing, most of us don't stop to think about why we're ailing. Perhaps it's because we don't believe that we really know or can figure out why. Perhaps it's because we do realize why we're sick and focusing on it might mean making life changes that we're uncomfortable with. In her book, Healing Your Body, author Louise H. Hay discusses the role that we play in our own healing process. She states:

The thoughts we have held and the thoughts we have repeatedly used have created our life experiences up to this point. Yet that is past thinking, we have already done that. What we are choosing to think and say, today, this moment, will create tomorrow and the next day, and the next week and the next month and the next year, etc. The point of power is always in the present moment. This is where we begin to make changes.

The energy required to tell a lie to yourself or to other people, hold on to painful memories, foster a hostile disposition, generate anger in yourself or someone else, or cling to insecurities about who you are is all negative. There is nothing positive about carrying emotional baggage from one relationship to the next or repressing your pain through self-destructive behavior. When you choose to generate such negative energy, you put your emotional and spiritual well being at risk. You may already realize that. If you can

111

accept that negative energy has an adverse effect on your emotional and spiritual health, there is no reason to believe that your physical health has been spared. Think about it for a moment. When you introduce a food substance, chemical material, or any "foreign matter" into your body, it immediately gives you a signal. If what you've done is enhancing to your body, it tells you so by sending pleasurable signals such as a feeling of satisfaction or relief. If what you've done is toxic, your body also sends you a signal. That signal could be anything from expelling the food through vomiting to any number of "allergic" reactions. If you are like most people, you have learned to translate what you have done to mean that it is either physically beneficial or detrimental to you.

Using the same logic, think about how your body physically changes under certain emotional conditions. For example, what happens to you physically when you tell a lie, get caught, then try to lie your way out of the first lie? Does your heart race? Does your breathing become deeper or faster? Do your palms sweat? Does your head seem to pound? How about when you lose control of your anger and become combative? Do you feel out of sorts or off balance? Those knots in your stomach and sledge hammer in your head is your body's way of telling you that a toxin is present. Your body is trying to signal to you that something is not right. In a way, your body's trying to protect you from yourself. For many of us, listening to our bodies comes after we can associate our physical discomfort to a mechanical cause, such as when our muscles hurt after a workout or when our heads ache from loud noises. Fortunately, our bodies don't only scream at us for relief because of the physical effort we exert. Our bodies are also the receptacles of our spiritual and emotional energy, too. When we introduce information into our systems that is spiritually and emotionally toxic, our bodies send up a red flag. You may not want to or believe that you know how, but you can heal yourself!

112

SELF-SURVEY
AM I LEARNING FROM MY MISTAKES?

1. If I really care for someone, I expect that person to live up to my standards and to change if necessary.

2. I seem to be attracted to the same type of man even though none of my past relationships with that type have lasted very long.

3. I'm too embarrassed to talk with my teenage daughter about sex, even though I know that she's interested in boys.

4. I don't usually monitor what my children watch on television. After all, they have to learn about real life sooner or later.

5. Where I work, the last person who was late 3 times in a row was fired, but that won't happen to me because I have good excuses whenever I'm late.

6. During an argument, my boyfriend hit me, but it was my fault for making him so mad.

7. My neighbors are always peering out of their windows at my house. I should really give them something to see.

8. My best friend is terrible with managing her money. So I usually make loans to her when she needs it.

9. My boyfriend asked me to marry him. Even though I don't love him, I said yes. I'm sure that I'll grow to love him.

10. A person with an addiction won't change unless s/he hits rock bottom.

113

CHAPTER *FIVE*

Your Man: Friend or Foe?

To realize that you do not understand
is a virtue.
Not to realize that you do not understand
is a defect.

From the second that he is born, to the moment that he is old enough to understand the spoken word, to the instant the he draws his last breath of life, the Black male is told by America that he has no worth. He is forced to view himself through the eyes of his oppressors as a subhuman being simply on the basis of the color of his skin. After months, years, and even decades it becomes too hard for some Black men not to believe what everyone, everywhere seems to maintain. This is why so many Black men give up. They stop caring about themselves. They are unable to love themselves. It can take a long time for a Black man to be stripped of his self-worth, but eventually it can happen. It is an insidious campaign from which many Black men fall. It does not happen to *all* of them, but it happens to enough of them to upset the fragile cultural balance that sustains Black Americans as Americans.

The emergence of Black women as fully capable and competent is a long time in coming. At first, the problem seemed to be that some Black women had been "sleeping" while their men managed their lives and their futures. By the time these women awoke, their men were gone. Lost to drugs, lost to an unjust penal system, lost to the "allure" of White women, even lost to other men. It was almost as if these Black men were stopped in their tracks while their Black women continued to march forward towards self-discovery. Now, it appears as though an entire generation of Black American men continue to lag behind the women in this respect. Those Black men who are deaf to the rhetoric of this society seem scarce in number.

To complicate matters more, Black women are constantly having to cope with the so-called "shortage of appropriate Black men" in this country. The general pattern of rejection by Black women of Black men is creating such high levels of personal stress between them that their ability to accept one another as people is being jeopardized. Our survival as a race is dependent upon our ability to live with one another, accept one another, help one another, and to be able to rely on one another for support. As you make contact with Black men, there may be those who do not meet your expectations, requirements, or standards in general. However, a Black man who is not "right" for you still can be left with his dignity intact. The bashing and emotional castrating that some women engage in is doing irreparable damage to all Black men.

RECOGNIZING MR. RIGHT

What is secure is easily grasped.
What has no omens is easily forestalled.
What is brittle is easily split.
What is minuscule is easily dispersed.
Act before there is a problem;
bring order before there is disorder.

In the real world, there is no such thing as a perfect man. The "superman" who many Black American women dream of is little more than a fragment of their collective imaginations. It is impossible for any man of flesh and blood to compete with that. If you are a single Black woman, you no doubt have an idea of your "ideal" man in your mind. It would not be fair, reasonable, or realistic for you to expect a real person to, without faults or deficiencies. After all, you are not. All too often, Black women assess the worth of their men according to standards that were manufactured by persons who do not have their best interests at heart.

For example, many Black women insist that their men be as flawless and chiselled as the men in the blue jeans commercials who get "made up" to look perfect. They want their men to drive expensive sports cars like their favorite movie stars who are given sports cars to drive. They expect their men to look suave and debonair all of the time like the models in magazines who are placed in poses and told how to look. They demand that their men be fearless like the heros in the movies who have stunt doubles to take the real risks. They insist that their men be tireless like the professional athletes who are paid inflated salaries to play games. When real Black men do not live up to their fairy tale expectations, Black women are disappointed. Consequently, they reject the real men for the manufactured

116

ones. They accept an advertiser's version of what real manhood is, even though that depiction has nothing to do with reality.

Every time that a Black woman rejects a Black man on the basis of such standards, she helps to confirm in a thousand unspoken ways what America has been contending all along. That is, that Black men have no value in this society, are not capable of achieving any degree of valid greatness, and cannot even fulfill the needs of their own women. As a race, we cannot afford to let that happen. It all begins with you. You must come to know who Black men are. How they function in this society. What they really want. What they really need. How you fit in. Most important, you must be willing to accept what you learn and use what you learn to help them if and when they need it. Be accurate in your perceptions of them. Not as ideals, but as human beings. If you are going to reject a Black man, do it because he does not fit your definition of realistic compatibility. Not because he does not measure up to fairy tale standards.

If you become involved with a Black man and later discover that you are not physically, emotionally, intellectually, or financially compatible with him, you may have just cause to reconsider your relationship with him. That is provided that your assessment of your relationship with him is accurate. If you decide that you are physically incompatible with him, it may be because you do not share the same interests in physical activities. You may be a recreational athlete while he prefers to be a couch potato or vice versa. You may feel that he lacks the skills or endurance to satisfy you sexually. On the other hand, your desire for sex and intimacy may be less frequent than his. Those are reasonable concerns. Emotionally, he may have a more "laid back" personality, while you might be more "reactive" to situations. He may lack the ability to be diplomatic in certain situations or may be prone to abusive tantrums. On the other hand, you may lack the ability to cope with his emotional highs and lows. An emotional incompatibility is a reasonable concern.

Intellectually, he may not be as versed on topics that are of interest to you. He may not feel that he is the "college type," while you may be totally motivated to pursue higher education. On the other hand, he may already be at the graduate level of study, while you are content with a minimal level of formal education. An intellectual incompatibility is a reasonable concern. If you are financially incompatible, it may be because your "take home pay" is greater than his. Not many men (Black or otherwise) can cope well with a spouse whose earning power exceeds theirs. On the other hand, if your earning power is less, he may not feel that your income allows you to contribute equally to the household. A financial incompatibility is a reasonable concern.

The way that a man dresses or the car that he drives are not valid reasons for rejecting him. The fact that a Black man may not have the body of Carl Weathers, the voice of James Earl Jones, the moves of Michael Jordan, or the smile of Billy Dee Williams are not real reasons to reject him. Unless you live in a fantasy world, your contact will more than likely be with real Black men. Treat them like real men. Talk to them. Share with them. Decide who is right for you on the basis of what is realistic, not on what you fantasize about.

FRIENDSHIP: LOVE INCOGNITO

As magnanimous as being in love is, the truest love usually springs from humble beginnings. The calm before the storm in human love affairs is what we call "friendship." The term may not bring to mind the kind of love that sends you reeling into psychotherapy, inspires cinematic greatness, or moves poets to plunge from bridges without bungee cords, but it is *real*. Without friendship, real love cannot happen because like anything of substance, it requires a

118

strong foundation. Friendship is that foundation. It is the foundation on which lasting love can be built. Love is little more than a self-directed journey. Like any journey, it begins with a first step. Friendship is that first step.

It seems unfair that the term "friendship" is often used to suggest a person's secondary importance. Sometimes when we say that a person is "just a friend," we do that to define the relationship as platonic and without sexual intimacy. Friendship often becomes the consolation prize when we announce that we "only want to be friends." So, due to our devaluing of friendships between men and women, it has become a greatly underated position to hold. That might not be the case if people took the time to consider the real value of being and having a friend. We get romanticized versions of the kind of relationships that are most "natural" for men and women to promote from television. Many of us accept those versions as valid. When we do, we give far more credence to those experiences that are sensual in nature rather than those whose basis is spiritual.

Friendship is love incognito. Between real friends there is a willingness to share, emotional support, sincere interest in one another, tolerance of each other's frailties, mutual respect, consistent loyalty, avid encouragement, dependability, and genuine warmth. All of these gifts are voluntarily exchanged between friends with clarity and honesty. What better prerequesites to romantic love could there be? In terms of intimacy, making love with your friend and being made love to by your friend is one of the greatest expressions of selfless love that two people can make. When friends choose to create a sexual union between them, they are able to view their intimacy not as a fusing of two wholes, but rather as a blending of two halves to make a whole.

Without friendship there would be chaos. Without friendship we would be left to our own primal devices to unravel the mysteries of love. In these modern times of intense fatal attractions and deadly sexual encounters, our ability to form mature partnerships with one another is crucial. Not every person that we meet can be a real friend to us. We cannot possibly be expected to be a real friend to everyone who enters our circle. That fact is what allows us consciously to choose to whom we give ourselves and our love. One of the wonderful things about being alive is that each day brings with it the opportunity to love someone other than and in addition to ourselves. All too often we take friendship for granted and forget that friendship is one of the most significant choices that we can make. We cannot choose our gender or select our biological parents. We cannot pick who our brothers and sisters will be. We cannot choose our race. We cannot choose the circumstances into which we are born or the physical form that our bodies will take at the moment of our conception and birth. We cannot choose many of the factors that serve to shape who we are, but we can choose our friends.

We can choose who we will give ourselves, our trust, and our love to. *Love does not choose us. We choose love.* As difficult as it may be for some people to believe, love does not come for us like some thief in the night. It is not something that springs up out of nowhere or catches us off guard. While it may sometimes be misdirected by us, it is not something that is without a predetermined course. We are all born with the ability to love. The proof of that is in the friendships that we strive to build and the friends we strive to become. Friendship between men and women is romantic love in its most subtle form. Friendship is the test drive that precedes the long haul that we all want to make with a significant other. Friendship is what puts us at ease and helps to reduce the anxieties that can come with being ourselves in front of an audience.

THE DESTRUCTIVE POWER OF HIDDEN AGENDAS

Wouldn't it be wonderful if what we didn't know couldn't hurt us? Of course, that old adage is far from true. What we don't know can and usually does hurt us. Even though we have the ability to reveal and detect our desires on a variety of levels, not knowing the truth damages us. All of us have been trained to conceal parts of our inner selves. We do it because we believe it to be in the interest of self-preservation. We do it because it is familiar and comfortable and we are creatures of comfort. We do it because we are afraid of newness and discomfort. We do it because we believe that we have to do it in order to maintain that sense of familiarity and comfort that we crave. We do it so much that doing it has become automatic. However, just because our preference for camouflage is automatic, it doesn't mean that it isn't conscious. We know that we do it. We know when we do it. We know why we're doing it.

When we camouflage the most precious parts of our being, our vantage point becomes one that limits our choices. We stifle our ability to ask for what we need by focusing instead on what we want. We cripple our ability to say what we are feeling by revealing only what we are thinking. We disrupt our ability to admit and give into our pain by only acknowledging our joy. According to Dr. Marlin S. Potash, author of *Hidden Agendas*:

When we recognize what our real needs are, what our true feelings are, and what is genuinely painful to us, but choose not to make them known to other people, we have a hidden agenda. That hidden agenda revolves around what we believe our comfort zones to be. We use hidden agendas to get what we want without saying that we want it. When we wear the camouflage that hidden agendas provide, we hope that people will see us the way we want to be seen. Instead, this camouflage affects the way that we see things. When we use a hidden agenda to solve a problem, the way we see a problem is the problem.

For example, we see ourselves as unhappy. Yet we do not generate the positive energy that we can to ensure happiness for ourselves. We see our personal relationships as restricting. Yet, we do not convey that we can manage freedom responsibly. We see our mates as people who limit their trust in us. Yet, we do not behave as though we can be totally trusted. We create our own circumstances. We propel ourselves into experiences that are fueled by the positive and negative energy that we supply them.

Hidden agendas require a tremendous amount of negative energy in order to be sustained. The energy required to maintain a lie can never be positive even if that lie is perpetuated for "good reasons." If a situation requires truth in order to be resolved and you respond with deceit, it doesn't matter why deceit was chosen. What matters in terms of spiritual growth is that the lie was chosen. The human spirit cannot afford such negative expenditures of energy. As fragile as we are, we sometimes underestimate our own resiliency. We will heal from the truth even if that truth is painful to us. Lies are what leave permanent scars because they tear into the soul.

SAMPLER OF BLACK MEN

When you wish to contract something
you must momentarily expand it.
When you wish to weaken something
you must momentarily strengthen it.
When you wish to reject something
you must momentarily join with it.
When you wish to seize something
you must momentarily give it up.
This is called "subtle insight."

Black men come in a variety of shapes, sizes, and hues. Aside from the cultural and racial identification that they have, their vocations and occupations also help to create their identities. The creativity, ingenuity, and overall adaptability of the Black man is an historical fact. Their attributes were realized very early into their arrival to America and quickly became survival skills. They invented labor-saving devices that helped to reduce the probability of being worked to death by their captors. They made agricultural breakthroughs that allowed them to make full use of the land's gifts. They made medical discoveries that served to save and preserve life. Throughout history, Black men have proven that they can become whatever they choose to become in spite of the obstacles.

You will meet many Black men who strive to achieve personal, financial, and spiritual greatness. You will also meet many Black men who do not. It should not have to be so hard to be a Black man in America, but it is. The hardships of Black men can be lessened by the support from Black women. In order to give that support, it is necessary to look at what has become of Black men and how the American society has affected them.

CORPORATE ONES

If one is as cautious at the end
as at the beginning
there would be no failure.

Corporate America does not embrace the Black man. It *tolerates* his participation because it recognizes his revenue-generating potential. America is a purely profit-driven country that knows Black men can make money for it. The Black man will probably never be welcomed into the corporate "boys club." However, most Black men already know this. Still, this does not prevent them from taking their perceived role in corporate America very seriously. From their Oxford shirts to their Brooks Brothers shoes, these Black men are ready and willing to play the "ultimate thinking-man's game."

Black corporate men are nothing short of amazing. They have succeeded in creating and maintaining a tiny, yet powerful, subculture that dictates the behavior of large numbers of people. Within this subculture they have created their own language, their own set of rules and regulations, and their own systems for rewards and punishment. They are not just pencil pushers. These Black men are the oil that make the machinery work. They are also, to a large degree, valuable mediators for their White colleagues. They act as a link between the Black communities and the rest of the corporate world. They promote products and ideas not just for the White world, but for the Black world as well. Black Americans have money. That is a fact. There may not be as many Black people with money as there are White, but Black people have significant earning and spending power. Blacks in the corporate world know and appreciate this. They recognize that Black empires can be built just as readily as White empires.

124

Those Black men who achieve success within the sub-culture of the corporate world do so because they learn from example. They learn from the successes and failures of those businessmen who have come before them. They take a systematic approach that starts by defining success and focusing on what they equate it to be for them. They decide on what their professional parameters will be. That is, on what they will and won't do for the sake of success. Black corporate "players" realize right away that initially they will have to work twice hard as for half as much. They can accept that as fact yet keep their focus on the brass ring.

If a Black man believes himself to be a member of the corporate family, he can adopt its ideals without regret. He simply modifies the terms of his membership to accommodate his individual temperament and value system. Not all Black corporate men are as cold and calculating as that world perpetuates (although many of them are). Not all of them are reconciled to the "business is business" philosophy. Those who are not are still able to meet their career objectives without being sinister. They are objective men who allow for subjective influences. They have feelings about the jobs that they do and can take a far less mechanized approach to completing them as their White colleagues might. These Black men are not totally motivated by greed, although it does factor in to some degree. They have the desire to improve the quality of their lives, but are also in sync with the other lives that will be affected in the process. These men are able to meet their career objectives with enthusiasm and creativity. Such Black men make ideal mentors and mates for self-actualizing Black women because they share several of the same traits. They are both driven to excel, yet can remain principled during their pursuit of excellence. They are efficient in their methods while sensitive to external factors. Together, this Black couple can achieve great things because they have vision, a firm belief in possibilities, and a willingness to work for and earn their rewards.

Naturally, the corporate world also enlists Black men with less noble motivations. These men better exemplify the common opinion of businessmen. They are extremely proficient at "playing the game" and have patterned themselves after their professional mentors (who could be Black or White). These Black men take a certain amount of pride in the clones that they have become. Some of them subscribe to the notion that they have found a way to escape the fate that is all too typical of Black men. They believe that they deserve better and ultimately are better than their Black brothers and sisters.

As a Black woman, you have met this corporate clone before. He will only wear "certain" clothes. Every piece of clothing that he owns, from his suits to his briefs, must bear a designer's label. He insists that his wardrobe make a statement about the superior man that he believes himself to be. He will only drive a "certain" make and model car because he believes that an automobile is a true reflection of his superior lifestyle and taste. He will only date "certain" women. It is a safe bet that White women are high on his list of candidates. He wouldn't dream of having a woman on his arm who did not confirm his superior level of physical attractiveness and virility. He believes that a man should be judged by the company he keeps. So, he limits his traveling to exclusive social circles. In order for you to be a member of his club, he will have to be convinced that you share the same criteria for dressing, socializing, and judging other people as he does. He has drawn a very rigid line of demarcation around himself, allowing only a "privileged few" to cross over it. He will expect you to do the same.

As a businessman, he is excellent. At least in the empirical sense because he systematically translates everything into dollars and cents. As a person, you may find him to be a materialistic, narcissistic, unscrupulous, opportunistic jerk who uses his feelings of superiority to justify his total lack of regard for basic human rights and equality. He can probably be convinced to put the screws to anyone for the right price. The best thing that you can do is prevent him from doing that to you.

YOUR PLACE IN CORPORATE AMERICA

To say that the corporate world is not receptive to women would be a gross understatement. About the only thing worse than being a Black person seeking entrance is being a Black female seeking entrance. The "good old boy" attitude reigns supreme in the corporate world. That attitude perpetuates the notion that the last thing the business world needs is a Black woman trying to move in on a White man's territory. Corporate White men have determined the "proper" place for their own women and have deemed a Black woman's position to be several levels below that. So, as a Black woman you will be expected to prove yourself in ways that no White woman or Black man could possibly imagine.

Overt sexual and racial discrimination will be commonplace. The range of offenses against you will be anything from having to "fetch" coffee for your male colleagues to allowing "accidental" intimate contact in crowded elevators to dismissing the "harmless" flirtation from your male superiors to coping with direct solicitation of sexual favors from those in positions of power. The obstacles that present themselves to Black women in the corporate world have the potential to totally destroy your character, self-esteem, and values system. Sadly, they won't all be delivered by White men. Occasionally there may be a Black corporate clone who will need to flex his corporate muscles at your expense. If you are forced to maintain a working relationship with him, you will have to decide whether or not to play the game or go around him in order to meet your career objectives.

If you decide to play along with him, try to limit your play to strategic maneuvers that will not incite conflicts.

That may sound like an enormous feat, but you are just as smart as he is. Probably more so. Understand deceit, but choose to be honest. Understand manipulation, but choose not to be destructive. If you choose not to play along with him, prepare yourself for a conflict. A man scorned can be just as treacherous as a woman. You have legal rights that are supposed to protect you from men such as this one. Exercise your rights, but do not be naive enough to think that "whistle blowing" will be taken graciously. Before things get to that point, you might try to resolve the matter without intervention. Give this man a clearly defined choice. That may be an effective strategy. When you give a person choices you are also giving that person a sense of control. Tell him how inappropriate his behavior is. Don't assume that he knows that. Give him the choice of either correcting his behavior or facing the legal consequences of that behavior. If he chooses the latter, help should only be a telephone call away. Do not allow this man or any other male coworker to harass you a second time. Stand up for your rights by getting help. A sad thing about this harassment scenario is that you and the Black male presented here probably have similar career goals. You could be working as a team.

The difference between the two of you is the way you go about achieving them. Playing the corporate game well means learning how and when to circumvent or get around someone and knowing who is ultimately responsible for what. One of the skills that you must master in the corporate world is that of listening. The ability to listen to others and *really hear* what they are saying will prove invaluable because as a Black woman you will find that few people will talk directly to you. Most will tend to talk at you as though you were a non-person. As you listen to others, try to develop a sensitivity to what is *not* said as well as to what is said. As your listening skills sharpen, you may be able to fend off attacks on your abilities and credibility as a member of the corporate community.

128

Your success within the corporate world can also be hampered by other Black women. There may be a significant number of them who cannot understand your drive to succeed in this arena. Not all of them will be your coworkers. Some of these Black women will be family members and persons from your inner circles. They lack sympathy for your "plight," and will encourage you to pursue a less masculine interest or suggest that you find something more "appropriate" to do with your life. Don't let it discourage you. Their constant reminders of your place as a Black woman may overwhelm you at times. However, such comments will come from Black women who cannot accept that you could be a catalyst for change because they have chosen to remain immersed in their own fears and failures. You can make it in the corporate world or any world that you choose to enter. The work will be harsh, the hours will be long, the opposition will be great, but the rewards will be even greater. Everything that you have ever dreamed of having or becoming is out there waiting for you to make it happen.

HELPLESS ONES

I dare not be a host,
but rather be a guest.
I dare not advance an inch,
but instead retreat a foot.

The most important thing to remember about this Black man is that *he chooses to be what and who he is.* The reasons for his choices may never be made clear to you. But, nevertheless, only he is responsible for them. This Black man is very needy and quite helpless in many ways. His needs extend themselves far beyond those that are material in nature. He may very well have all of the material possessions that he wants or requires. His greatest needs are more

129

spiritual in nature. This man chooses to be oblivious. He is not a fighter in any sense of the word. He will avoid any kind of confrontation or conflict even if it means sacrificing himself or those experiences that would truly make him happy. It is not that he is necessarily unwilling to assert himself. He would if he believed that he could, but he doesn't. His passivity about his fundamental right to happiness is maddening to a person of your ideals. Unlike you, he finds little wrong with being the "lamb to the slaughter."

For him, the route that he has chosen to take in his life is the safest, calmest one. He would never consider allowing his personal happiness to interfere with the happiness of others. He will see to that even if it means appearing subservient and "wimpy." He needs a lot from everyone in his inner circle and he takes a lot from them because he does not believe that he can get those things for himself. Don't let his looks fool you. There may be no physical or physiological reason why he is so inept. His looks will probably appeal to you. We won't necessarily be physically or socially awkward. If he were, you might at least be able to tolerate (in part) his low level of self-esteem. He may have a good job and a comfortable home. He may be free of any chemical dependencies. All in all, he may seem like a regular guy in many ways. He'll probably have friends who take an interest in him, recreation to entertain him, and income to sustain him. Still, you will sense that something is missing from this man.

The clues to who this Black man is will come when you ask him about his aspirations. He won't have any. When you ask him about his plans for the future, he won't have any of those, either. When you talk with him about the struggles of Black Americans, he will accuse you of being too idealistic and perhaps of being unreasonable. He may not come right out and admit it, but the better parts of his self-worth are immersed in feelings of doubt and limited to the parameters set by the very people who make him feel so

130

worthless. He does not believe in possibilities for his race or for himself. It is his hidden belief in his inferiority that makes him so helpless. Some people will argue that all this Black man needs is a "good" Black woman by his side. What this Black man needs is professional help! The feelings that this man has about himself did not happen over night. It had to have taken a long time for him to learn to hate himself. If he has managed to carry his feelings of inferiority from childhood to adulthood, it will take a great deal more than a good woman to correct his thinking. Even if it were within your powers to motivate this man, he would eventually drain you. Such a parasitic relationship would only impede your growth and jeopardize your chances of realizing your own goals.

This man will prove himself almost too easy to manipulate and control. It will be especially easy for a woman. If that woman is his mother, it will not matter if she is possessive, overbearing, or insensitive to his needs. In his eyes, she is his mother and what she says goes. He is not necessarily a "momma's boy," but his mother's umbilical cord will have an extremely long reach. If the female is his wife or live-in lover, he will feel obligated to adhere strictly to his vows or agreements even if they no longer have validity for him. It will not matter how incompatible or unhappy he is with his spouse or lover. He will not risk confronting her with *his right* to happiness. If their union has produced children, this man will be even less willing to fight for his own happiness and peace of mind. He will avoid confrontations by focusing his energies totally on his children. This way, he can use his children as a means of escape and as justification for perpetuating his fraudulent relationship. This man is subservient to almost everyone. He aims to please and he does. He has so little love for himself that he can completely ignore his needs as a person and as a man. He offers little resistance to routine and regimentation. He prefers to be told what to do because it relieves him of the burden of having to take responsibility for his actions. If everything is laid out for him, he'll behave according to the requirements of the "role." Since he succumbs very easily to guilt, he will probably not have a strong enough constitution to withstand the wrath of a significant person who has become displeased with him.

He considers himself to be a responsible person because he does what is expected of him. He is the consummate actor who would rather play out his assigned roles in life than seek discovery or fulfillment. If he is a married man, he will "act" like a husband is supposed to act. If he has a girlfriend, he will "act" like a boyfriend is supposed to act. To his parents, he will "act" like a good son is expected to act. To his superiors at work, he will "act" like a subordinate. If he holds a position in management, he will "act" like a boss. He is so predictable that you can almost set your watch by him. The only problem is that this man is "acting." He has so little self-esteem that he requires almost constant reassurances that he is doing the "right" thing in the eyes of other people. He is far more concerned with the approval of others than with self-approval. He is so accustomed to compromising his desires for the desires of other people that he may seem to be totally without drive or imagination.

As tempted as you may be to do it, *do not discard this man*. He can teach you a lot about yourself. One of the hardest things for you to do will be to accept him. After all, this is not a Black man who is incapable of great love and compassion. This is not a Black man who does not at least recognize the greatness in others. This is not a Black man who will not acknowledge who you are and the process through which you are going. This is a Black man who has sentenced himself to a kind of spiritual prison. For him it is a life sentence with no possibility for parole or escape. This is a Black man who firmly believes that he does not "measure up" to anyone's standards. He could be designing cars instead of tuning them. He could be building office complexes instead of cleaning them. He has an inventive mind, a curious nature, and an aptitude for many things. Like you, he has been endowed with many gifts, but he chooses to dismiss them.

From his perspective, you may represent the proverbial "serpent" in what he believes is his garden of Eden. If so, you are probably simultaneously terrifying and exciting. It is hard to say whether the fear of *what you do to him* is greater than the fear of *what you do for him*. He may be scared to death by how exhilarated he is by you. He may even play little self-control games when he is with you because he does not believe that he "deserves" to feel as good as he does when he is with you. Perhaps you incite feelings of desperation in him that force him to acknowledge the total lack of control that he has over his life.

In addition to being afraid of himself, he also fears women. Especially strong Black women. He lives in constant fear of having to deal with them even though he relies so heavily on them for his salvation. One of the few times when his fears are lessened may be while he is engaged in sex with them. It may be one of the limited ways in which he can "assert" himself without risking disapproval. That is, providing that he believes himself to be a satisfying lover. Given all of the "flaws" that this helpless Black man possesses, he is still able to admire and respect you. Perhaps he believes that you are all the things that he is not or could ever be. However, this man would probably not have the spiritual strength to survive a romantic relationship with you. Even if you were able to expand your mind far enough to motivate the genius that sleeps inside of him, he would only deplete the better parts of you.

LIBERAL ONES

Always be without desire,
in order to observe its wondrous subtleties.
Always have desire,
so that you can observe its manifestations.

The practice of interracial dating and marriage is a source of resentment and frustration for many Black women. You may even have such feelings. There are some people who believe that "race mixing" is inappropriate, unacceptable, and ultimately unforgivable. However, you will have to come to terms with any negative feelings that you have about this practice. Even if you have been personally rejected by a Black man for a White woman. Interracial relationships between Black men and White women are begun and severed every day. It would be self-destructive for you to focus on factors that are out of your control. The attraction that some Black men have to White women is one of those factors. You may not agree with the practice of interracial dating and mating, but your personal growth may be affected by any inability on your part to cope with it.

There are a variety of reasons aside from physical attraction why a Black man might select a Caucasian woman or any woman not "of color." One theory that has been offered is that the Black man has forgotten that not too long ago, Black men were lynched over the very *possibility* of doing what he is doing now. Simply the thought of a Black man "coupling" with a White woman has cost many of our ancestors their lives. Any Black man who dared to commit such a "crime" against the White race paid the ultimate price. It was not only acceptable then, but encouraged to murder any Black man found guilty of having the desire or intent to mix with a White woman. Race mixing meant an

134

automatic death sentence for the Black man, but those Black men were not the only victims. Black women also lost their husbands, fathers, and sons to the paranoia of Whites.

Few people in America are truly color blind with respect to adult relationships. America does not promote the color blind mindset and is very blatant about the distinctions it chooses to make between peoples. Any Black man who grows up in America already knows this. Black women know this too. That is perhaps one reason why Black women might view the decision of some Black men to cross over racial lines as a "symptom" of a larger problem. Given the degree and complexity of the attempts that some people have made to devalue Black men in general, a low self-esteem is frequently viewed as the real motivating factor behind interracial dating and mating. Few of us are in the position to make professional clinical judgments about the psychological dynamics of interracial dating. However, some Black women are astute enough to suspect that reasons outside of mere physical or sexual attraction compel some Black men to pass them over for White women. Low self-esteem is just one of them.

Contrary to what many people might believe, low self-esteem is not a condition indigenous to Black people. Any person of any race can harbor feelings of worthlessness. Black people may have been singled out because of the "fear response" that has been bred into many of them. Being taught to fear can also give rise to feelings of diminished worth. Typically, persons with low self-esteem will often look to others for feelings of worth in themselves. These people also seem unable to cope with being challenged or with failing to meet a challenge. A Black man who suffers from this condition might demonstrate its symptoms in a variety of ways. That includes, but is not limited to, boosting his self-perceptions by turning to White women.

This society has a way of exposing Black men to their

worst fears. Perhaps as a means of self-preservation, many Black men are attracted to pursuing relationships that will not cause them to feel fearful or anxious. Black men typically do not fear White women. They fear White men. Black men have learned to fear White men because White men have come to symbolize power and authority. To the average Black man, the White man is the police who watches him, the lawyer who defends him, and the judge who sentences him. White women pose no immediate threat to Black men. Black men know that they have nothing to fear from White women. Given the climate in this country, removing or minimizing the element of fear from any relationship makes that relationship more of a probability for a Black man. If you understand that reasoning, then the actions of a Black man are not nearly as important as the reasons for his actions.

There are many Black women who understand the complexities of interracial dating. Perhaps they understand those dynamics better than Black men. Black women are also victims of the overt racism and paranoia that has come to symbolize White America because they feel powerless to effect change. They feel powerless against the attraction of their men to "forbidden fruit." The pain coupled with the resentment of being passed over for a White woman is not something that can be easily managed.

If a Black man who prefers White women has not forgotten the price that was paid for the "past sins" of his forefathers, perhaps he is exercising what he believes is a form of power that was previously unavailable to him. Maybe, somewhere in the back of his mind, is the notion that "taking" a White woman will somehow allow him to get revenge against White men. Perhaps he may feel that having a White woman would be a far more serious blow to the White race than any other action he could take. Although it would be difficult to prove, self-hate is a theory that is gaining increasing popularity. It also has been theorized that

Black men who reject Black women do so because of a history of failed relationships with them. Some have suggested that Black men who practice interracial dating and mating do so because they have become disillusioned with Black women and make generalizations about their incompatibility. The concerns that many Black women have about liberal Black men are probably similar to those of women from other nationalities whose men turn to women outside of the race.

The fact that some Black men choose to cross over racial boundaries to find a mate is a reality. However, this practice does not appear to be the norm. A Black woman can still find a significant number of Black men who reject the idea that women outside of their race can add anything of real substance to their lives. They are not Black men who are liberal in their thinking and seem repulsed by the thought of any type of intimacy occurring between Black man and White women. They would probably not be able to understand what would motivate a proud Black man to turn his back on an eligible Black woman. These non-liberals consider themselves to be culturally committed Black man and tend to view interracial dating and marriage as insulting to the Black culture in general. They focus so intently on the racial and cultural differences that exist between peoples that they refuse to do anything that might compromise their cultural philosophies. They are not racists; they mean no ill will to any race. They are not implying superiority over other races. They simply cannot condone certain types of mingling between them.

Obviously not all Black men are committed to such a strict cultural code. There are some who behave as though they believe that all women are created equal and that a woman is a woman no matter what her race or ethnic background. Perhaps these men believe that the differences between women are subtle ones or ones exclusive to their individual personalities. Liberal Black men might say that it is no more advantageous being with a White woman than it is being with a Black woman and vice versa. They might claim to give more credence to basic human relationships. If that attitude is sincere, these Black men will give new meaning to the term "color blind." A Black man who is sincerely blind to color differences might focus more on finding his "soul mate" than on finding a woman to mate from his own race. Perhaps in his heart, Ms. Right has no color. He may be secure enough in his abilities as a person and as a man that racial politics won't be the primary grounds for stepping outside of his race to find her.

In many ways a Black man who dates White women is just like a Black man who does not. That is, he'll have friends who enjoy him, coworkers who respect him, a family who supports him, and Black women who desire him. When you meet this man, he may not mention to you that his wife or girlfriend is not a Black woman. That might not be because he is trying to hide it from you. He may simply prefer not to make an "issue" out of it. When he speaks about his "better half" to you, he may limit that conversation to testimonials about her qualities as a person. Perhaps he will mention some of the things that make them compatible as friends or even lovers. He may talk about how fulfilled he is at having met her. The fact that she is Anglo Saxon, Asian, or any other person not of African descent may be of no real consequence to him. He might just be happy that he has finally found someone who he believes he can comfortably share his life with.

Sometimes you will find an outgoing and opinionated Black man coupled with a reserved and passive White woman. You should not be surprised to see this Black man continue to live a Black lifestyle outside of their interracial relationship. If that is the case, he will more than likely continue to socialize with his Black friends as well as pursue Black women. He may even have a Black woman "on the side" if he can get away with it. The passivity of his

138

White woman helps to convince him that he can continue to "be Black" as long as he does not have to sacrifice his White woman.

There are also those Black men who prefer that their White women be older than they are. Perhaps these men are relying on the White woman's fear of aging to motivate material and maternal generosity. If she owns an expensive car, has a "healthy" bank account, or maintains an independent life style, she will probably have little or no trouble attracting and holding on to a Black man who is receptive to being bought. Even an older White woman without the usual "trappings" may still appeal to a liberal Black man if she has the "seasoning" that he is looking for. His need to be with this type of woman may have a connection to the relationship that he has with his mother. Particularly if the interracial relationship appears to be strongly maternal in nature. If "mothering" is what this liberal man needs, he'll select a White woman who won't mind supporting him emotionally, sexually, and financially whenever necessary.

You may not agree with a liberal man's choices in a mate because they exclude your race, but you must respect his right to choose. There may be nothing underhanded about this man. There may be no hidden agendas. He may at first seem oblivious to the realities of this society, but upon careful scrutiny you may find that he has created a series of carefully placed "buffers." These buffers serve to protect him from those who might otherwise undermine his idea of what is right for him. He may have no desire to impose his beliefs on others. So, you may never actually meet his mate. If that is his pattern, he will continue his associations with his Black friends, but not include his White mate in many of those social affairs and gatherings. He will be very selective about their joint activities. This way, he gets to keep everyone happy and as comfortable as possible with his personal decisions. No one will be subjected to or forced to deal with it.

If he is basically a private person who chooses to make his personal affairs public, it could be for several reasons. It might be that he wants to rule out the possibility of anyone playing politics with his personal life. He may be trying to prevent others from using his personal choices against him. This Black man fully realizes that if given the opportunity, others less accepting of his decisions might be prejudiced against him. He wants to avoid problems.

Another reason could be that he wants other people to believe that he is free of shame or remorse about his decision. He may want to give the impression that (he believes) his choice in a mate is no less valid than the choices that other Black men (who do not date interracially) make. He may need to create comfort zones between himself and those persons with whom he regularly interacts. If there are family members, friends, or coworkers who oppose his choice in a mate, he will want to know who they are so that they can be dealt with accordingly. Once he has diffused all of the potentially volatile situations and relaxed the "hysteria," he can get on with the business of co-existence with his White mate.

You might consider not attaining this man as simply the luck of the draw. He probably did not set out in search of a White woman or any woman not of his race. He may have only wanted to find the right woman for him. In his search he discovered that racial and cultural differences don't have to prevent people from coming together. However, that discovery may not prevent him from pursuing a sexual or personal relationship with you. He may not have forgotten who he is, but if he seems too preoccupied with proving his Blackness, that might suggest a base line dishonesty that he has not dealt with. He may be in denial about his true motivations for being in an interracial relationship. If he is, he will do whatever it takes to exorcise the guilt that he feels about having selected a White woman as a mate.

If you can be a friend to this man, then do so. He needs

real friends, especially Black ones. He may not admit that he needs you, but he does. He may need to be told that he is not wrong about exercising his right to choose. He may need to be told that he is not a traitor to his race or a conspirator against his people. However, you must realize the impact that his individual choices have on the race as a whole even if he does not. Perhaps that impact might be something that he has failed to consider in his quest for the perfect mate. Wish him well, but move on. He is probably not of the state of mind to be converted back to his race since he may not feel that he has violated any natural laws by stepping outside of it.

You must recognize that it is not your right to impose your ideas or ideals on him in an attempt to institute change for your own gain or for the sake of your race. Ours is a strong race with a proven track record for survival. If this man believes that he is happy, then so be it. There is a lot that can be learned from him. At the very least, his discoveries will aid you in your quest for absolute understanding of the cultural differences that exist between peoples.

Of the Black men who practice interracial dating and marriage, a portion of them do it primarily for economic reasons. These men appear to be obsessed with proving themselves to the White world. You may have already met this man. He is well aware of his "assets," but not above occasionally exaggerating about them. As a communicator, he is proficient. The fact that he can "talk White" and "talk Black" leads him to believe that he is bilingual. Having this skill is part of what allows him to move in and out of both worlds with relative ease. He will probably be more versed in the affairs of White folks than of Black folks because he chooses to remain out of touch with his own people. Generally speaking, he considers himself to be successful in the White world because he uses what White people don't know about Black people to his advantage. He is very good at using their ignorance as a weapon against them.

Even with all of his intelligence and savvy, his thinking is seriously flawed. He has somehow deduced that there are greater advantages to having a White woman than with remaining with a Black woman. In essence, he denounces his race because he thinks that it is powerless and ineffective. He does not equate Black people with living well or having access to the finer things in life. To this person, there is no "prestige" in being a Black man in a White world unless he can possess an essential element of that world. Namely, their women. He considers White women to be the prize; a reward for a job well done. He believes that they are the catalysts for all of the doors that have been opened to him.

It will be fascinating to watch this man in operation. He will "woo" White women with confirmations of the much celebrated sexual prowess of Black men. He will find a way to appeal to their natural curiosity about him. Then, he will manipulate their curiosity by perpetuating any and all stereotypes that might possibly advance his cause. He tries to portray himself as close to White as Black can be. This type of liberal man is ready and willing to sell himself to the highest bidder. He embraces the rhetoric of this society as though it were a true reflection of his manhood.

Don't be surprised to see this Black man behave towards White women in ways that no self-respecting Black woman would tolerate. He may not hesitate to be verbally and/or physically abusive towards her in public. He may continue to come and go as he pleases without regard for their commitment. He may even carry on multiple sexual relationships with White and Black women. Do not accept this Black man's views on the "inadequacies" of his race. His reality vastly differs from yours. Money and prestige are his objectives. Since he will not recognize you as capable of providing him with either, you are automatically not a consideration as a mate. He knows full well what he is doing.

As a Black woman, all you can do is prevent him from doing anything to you. Since you may be only a subordinate in his eyes, all he may choose to do is take from you.

MARRIED ONES

What is firmly established
cannot be uprooted.
What is tightly embraced
cannot slip away.

Of all the relationships that you will have with Black men, those with married ones will be the most interesting and possibly the most beneficial to your personal growth. As you pursue your professional aspirations in traditionally male domains, such as business, science, medicine, or law, many of your coworkers will be male. A significant number of those males may be married. These married men will function as both superiors and subordinates and will not be without their own preconceived notions about your role as a Black woman. Some of your very best friends as well as your worst enemies will be married men.

In her book, *Anatomy of Love: The Natural History of Monogamy, Adultery, and Divorce,* author Helen E. Fisher contends that of the 853 cultures on record, only 16 percent of those cultures practice monogamy. The Western culture is in the minority. As "civilized" devotees to Western thought, Black men in America must often submit to the Western interpretation of courtship and marriage. Its significance in our culture remains to be seen since Western ideals frequently lack the richness and imagination that our heritage demands. It specifically does not allow for the unique styles of loving that Black men can offer to Black women. Since it is a fact that monogamy is more a sociological parameter than a biological requirement (in Western culture), the unions that Black couples promote need to be

143

forged from values that are relative to their experiences as men and women of African descent.

Love between human beings is not limited to romance and eroticism. Love can be platonic or paternal with any number of variations in between. Though they may not be able to express it or even care to acknowledge it, Black men have the capacity for loving on a variety of different levels. They can feel a kind of love for a number of women at the same time. In the real world, women are not just wives and mothers. They are also friends and coworkers. Unfortunately, a married man is expected to express and demonstrate all forms of his love to his female kin and one spouse. If he does not adhere to that requirement, all hell is likely to break loose.

If a wife mistrusts her husband's intentions towards another woman, she will become fearful that he will devote the same kind of attention to this woman as he does to her. This will be a difficult situation for the husband to defeat because the wife may feel that she is well within her rights to demand a monopoly on his time and affections. His husbandly behavior might never have indicated that she feel otherwise. If she does become disgruntled over his attention to other women, she will analyze not only the quantity, but also the quality of attention that he pays to other women. If she feels that his attentions are inappropriate, she may find some way to protest it.

One of her largest concerns might be that his "friendship" with one woman in particular might develop into something more sophisticated. Her protests of this possibility will include rallying against him with those other females who would most likely be sympathetic to her position and effective in her campaign (e.g., his mother or mother-in-law, the sisters of either spouse or surviving grandparents). However, even if the husband feels that his wife's stance is unwarranted or considers her reaction too radical, he may not openly oppose her. Instead, he might

144

resort to lying in an attempt to keep everyone happy. If so, he will do whatever it takes to avoid a conflict and to pacify his wife's suspicions even if that means pretending not to be interested in other women. He will do whatever it takes to avoid having to explain to his wife why he needs to be with someone in addition to her.

Generally speaking, married men tend to compare marriage to a form of social retirement. Being married automatically eliminates certain social activities. Their "close" relationships with females will be the first thing to go. The only way that you can become or remain a friend to this man is by promoting your friendship in a nonthreatening way. That is, by establishing feelings of comradery rather than romantic affection and by becoming an addition to his life rather than an escape from it. Few couples will take the time to offer their definitions of marriage to one another before the marriage ceremony occurs. Perhaps they believe that the marriage vows will cover all of the bases for them. Perhaps they believe that through marriage they can institute the changes that they desire in one another.

Realistically, marriage vows do not always allow for the expression of individual needs and desires. Marriage vows are "codes of conduct" that serve as a guide for how to behave. These codes may sound specific (i.e., the promise of fidelity), but they are often left to individual interpretation. Some women would consider a "good" married man to be one who has completely submitted to the literal interpretation of his marriage vows. If so, his approach to marital realities might allow him to compromise and reciprocate without too much difficulty. He might accept the initial romance and idealism with enthusiasm, but have no trouble with rolling up his sleeves to deal with the more fundamental aspects of the union. He might not be the most exciting man that a woman will ever meet and his structured temperament might seem boring, but he'll probably be made of the stuff that self-actualizing women dream of.

If he were a single man, his sense of devotion, responsibility, and consistency make him perfect marriage material.

There are plenty of Black married men who fit that description. As a mentor, he will prove to be unparalleled. It can be uplifting to know a man with a strong sense of commitment who chooses to play by the rules of marriage and views himself in a specific and relatively unchanging light. If he considers himself as "fixed," there can be little harm in that if he also views his marriage as a stabilizer and himself as steadfast. For some Black men, marriage is a "coming of age" or an indicator of maturity. For some married men, marriage means buckling down and becoming a responsible adult. It means denouncing the frivolous and immature impulses of their youth. Marriage can be the first significant adult act that some men have ever performed.

However, there may be a down side to Mr. Perfect Husband that revolves around generalities. Generally speaking, a man does not always marry the woman that he *wants*. That woman would probably prove herself to be too exotic, too explosive, and too uncontrollable to him. As a bachelor, he has no doubt known her and may have wanted her desperately, but would never consider marrying her. Instead, he marries the woman who he *needs*. The woman who can demonstrate a need for him. Sometimes, she is the proverbial "nubile bride." The woman who even in these modern times is still able to project an air of innocence that implies that some aspect of her being has remained untouched. This woman may be more conservative with the risks that she takes (than the woman he wants), have a less flamboyant style, and be far less daring. She may come from a family with traditional values and morals. What may be most important about this woman is that she can allow herself to need him even though she might be independent in the practical sense.

Most men (and some women) understand the difference between wanting and needing. For them, wanting and needing are two entirely different states of mind that must

146

be kept in check. A man who is considering marriage will choose the state of mind that he can best cope with. He might be driven to maddening heights of pleasure by the woman who he wants and still not marry her. If he does not truly believe that this woman can need those aspects of him that he is willing and able to share, he knows that he will not be able to co-exist with her. A man will not live beyond his emotional means. Of course, those means will vary from man to man. Still, a man needs to feel that he can live up to the expectations of the woman who he has chosen to spend the rest of his life with. He needs to feel that their attraction to and desire for one another will be lasting. He needs to feel that the relationship has the substance that makes marriages work. He will not risk his emotions or state of mind on a woman who he believes has only a temporary interest in him.

We all need to be needed. A Black man with the desire to marry is not necessarily looking for a woman "just like the one who married dear old dad." However, a woman who presents a responsible attitude, a tendency towards stability, and an element of predictability will have a far greater chance of being his wife than a woman who does not. He expects his potential wife to be there for him. To stand by his side. To be willing to compromise as much as he believes he is. To be willing to work as hard as he does at being a spouse. To assume a traditional role if need be. To bear his children, love his family, and need their life together as husband and wife.

The escalating divorce rate in this country seems to imply that far too many married couples fail to listen to and hear one another. Sadly, many Black women believe that if their husbands step outside of their marriage to fulfill a need that involves another women, that the need must be sexual. A simple, forgotten truth is that people have many sides. Not all of which are sexual in nature and not all of whose sides are erased by marriage. Any woman who expects her husband to lose general interest in other women *because he is her husband* is deluding herself. After all, women are people too. They are people with ideas, opinions, and skills. Should a man be punished because he appreciates the contributions that women outside of his marriage can make to his life? A married man's interest in other women does not have to be laced with sexual overtones. If he turns to another female, does it mean that he does not love his wife? Should he sever genuine friendships with other women because he is no longer a bachelor? Should he stop relying on women outside of his marriage for support and counsel because he is married? Should other points of view only come from his male friends? There are many reasons why a married man might step outside of his marriage to promote a relationship with another woman. It would be terribly unfair to assume that he has any dishonorable intentions by doing so.

Married people sometimes commit infidelities. That is a fact of married life. However, it is not an inevitability. If it seems so, it might be because of the sensationalism that is associated with marital faithlessness. Single people seem to have a morbid interest in marital indiscretions. Some married people have realistic concerns about the probability of it happening to them. Marital infidelities can occur for a number of reasons. An extramarital affair can take place even in a marriage that seems solid. On the other hand, marriages that defy the odds of success can continue for years without any episodes of adultery.

Marriage has the potential for meeting many of our needs, but it cannot meet all of them. If it could, there would be no need for activities outside of marriage like hobbies or professional pursuits. Married people are not immune to seduction. That fact seems to elude many married couples who find themselves faced with it. For instance, seduction can be of an economic nature. Black people are seduced every day by the mass media into buy-

148

ing products that they are told will enhance them or improve some aspect of their lives. As a result, they willingly spend disproportionately to their means. When parents buy expensive toys for their children or spend hundreds of dollars on designer clothes or foreign cars for themselves, they are (in part) giving in to a form of seduction.

The seduction that occurs between a married man and a woman other than his wife might not begin as sexual. It may translate into sexual terms for him later, but it does not have to start out that way. If a married man does choose to permit a sexual seduction to occur, that choice is still not an accurate barometer for the love that he feels for his wife. A man who loves his wife can still be seduced to have sex or an extramarital affair with another woman. If his interest in the *sensation* of being with that woman is allowed to sufficiently peak to a level that overrides his commitment to fidelity, he is a likely candidate for adultery. On the other hand, it would probably be more difficult to seduce a man who is still in love with his wife because the in love state of mind is such a potent one. The focus of a man in love is so intense that it would be extremely difficult to distract him.

So many marriages are severed because of physical infidelities. If it is the husband who has committed the indiscretions, the wife will be instantly hurt by her husband's inability to remain faithful to her. Comparatively speaking, there is a vast difference between having sex and making love. Unlike sex, lovemaking is a very sophisticated form of communication. Lovemaking is an exclusively human way for adults to talk with one another. For a man, making love is a far more emotional experience than women generally realize. Many women can sense when they are being made love to or when they are merely being sperm receptacles. They instinctively know the difference between a lover who has come to their bed to take from them and one who has come to give to them. It is this "upper hand" that allows a woman to determine the "rightness" of her sexual partner. When a man makes loves with a woman, he offers his emotions first and cannot be truly fulfilled unless there is a mutual emotional exchange. Love making is a powerful and moving experience that can simultaneously terrify and excite him. That might be why so many men seem to encourage having sex over making love with women. Love making is such an emotionally risky and draining undertaking. Having sex takes much less emotional energy.

Intimacy is one of the most powerful and necessary forms of communication to occur between married couples. Unfortunately, many of them make the mistake of dismissing the importance of intimacy as something merely synonymous with sexual intercourse. They limit their intimate moments to only those that will directly result in having sex with one onother. This attitude can cause problems later because it does not allow for the multitude of experiences that are genuine intimate moments. Genuine intimacy between married couples involves the expression of a wide range of thoughts, feelings, and emotions. It would be impossible to list them all because they are all unique as the individuals who express them. Needless to say, sexual intercourse is a component of intimate communication. However, intimacy can occur between two people without it.

Intimacy can range from the sharing of childhood fears to the exchange of sexual fantasies. While intimacy can be physical, sexual, mental, or verbal, it must always be consensual if it is to be positive. That is, it must be something both people want. Intimacy between two people is most bona fied when it is desired by both people. A man will seek intimacy as long as it is pleasant, nonthreatening, nurturing, and above all, pain-free. A man will not be motivated to share intimate moments with a woman if he believes that those times will be stressful to him. If that is the case, his logic will dictate that intimacy is something to be avoided.

When a man chooses to avoid intimate communication with his wife (rather than work towards resolving intimacy challenges), a domino effect is created. Eventually, all forms of communication between him and his wife become counterproductive and very toxic. Once the desire to bond in a spiritual way is gone, sexual desire soon follows. Once that is allowed to happen, sexual tension builds for both of them. Without a positive outlet for their sexual energies, they are left with the only options they believe are available. That is, to release their sexual energies in negative ways through bickering, arguing, complaining, criticizing, and even fighting with one another. These are conscious choices that they both make when neither is willing to invest the positive energy into resolving the intimacy issue. It is a painful time for both parties, but it is a pain that both parties allow.

Still this scenario is not always enough to prompt a married man to end his marriage. If so, he will consider adultery to be a viable and legitimate option for him. When a man chooses to be unfaithful to his wife, it is not always with the intent of divorcing her. If his marital role also revolves around his social position or financial stability, he will allow himself to lead a double life by engaging in a extramarital affair. His desire to preserve what he has will greatly decrease the probability of starting all over again with another woman. The older he is, the less motivated he will be to start from scratch. For this man, an extramarital affair serves only to "take the edge off" the unpleasantries he associates with being married. An affair makes his marriage more tolerable because it represents what he believes is a valid escape from the stresses he associates with being married to that particular woman. Depending on his priorities, resources, and level of fear, he can carry on an extramarital affair for many months without being discovered or confronted by his wife. In some cases, the wife may have knowledge or suspicions about her husband's infidelity and may choose not to address it. She may want to catch him in the act or gather so much damning evidence against him that the burden of dissolving their marriage will rest primarily on his shoulders. Such a wife might be more motivated by the legal and financial advantages of uncovering and proving her husband's adulterous lifestyle.

Although carrying on an extramarital affair can be problematic for the married man (not to mention for his wife), infidelity in itself is not the real problem. Infidelity is only a symptom of the problem. The real problem is one that stems from negative communication and issues about intimacy that have not been properly addressed. If the marriage has produced children, an entirely different set of problems are created. The most common reason that married men give for remaining in unhappy marriages is their children. Many of them believe that it is their duty to stay in the home for the sake of the children no matter how unhappy that home is. A married man may believe that he is fulfilling his parental obligation by being a present father (instead of an absent one). However, this unhappy union with his wife fosters a dysfunctional environment in his home that his children have daily exposure to. If his home environment is painful and toxic to him, it stands to reason that it is also painful and toxic to his children. While he struggles to survive in an environment that is dysfunctional for him for the sake of normality, he is sending a dangerous message to his children. When children are reared in a home where mommy and daddy don't touch, don't kiss, don't smile, and don't like each other, those children see that as normal. It isn't normal. He is not only teaching his children that it is normal to be in a dysfunctional home, he is also teaching them to become dysfunctional adults.

Wives expect their husbands to confine the expression of their lust and desire to the parameters of their marital relationship, and rightly so. Their exchange of marriage vows was a solemn promise between. However, as distasteful as it sounds, at some point in his married life, a man may desire another woman. Whether or not he follows through with his desire is another matter.

Even a man with a strong bond to his wife can be enticed into giving in to his desire for another woman. Not all married men will "cheat" on their wives, but the potential for all of them to is there. A needy man can be a potent magnet to a problem-centered woman. The desire to "fix" what is broken in his life can be overwhelming. Still, it is important to remember that the same man who chose to get married is also choosing to stay married. If his happiness and peace of mind were as important to him as he may think it is, he would not stay in *any* situation that threatened it. That includes a marriage. If during your relationship with him you present yourself as merely a distraction from his marital responsibilities, then you run the risk of being treated as just that: a distraction. He might seem to you to be a sensitive and patient person. Perhaps if he directed his sensitivity and patience towards his wife, he might not have marital problems. He might seem to you to be honest and compassionate. Perhaps if he invested the same energy into showing honesty and compassion to his wife that he does in showing it to you, there would be no need for him to cry on your shoulder about his troubles at home.

Although everyone is different, there is one thing that holds true for all married men who are unfaithful to their wives: They're lying to someone! A cheating husband will sacrifice what he can't let go of in order to keep what he doesn't have. In other words, if he chooses to keep his marriage "intact," being with you will always be a "conditional choice" that he makes. If being with you compromises the appearance of marital stability too much, he will sacrifice the opportunity to be with you in order to sustain the lie that he is living. The fact of his shared intimacies with you means that he has forsaken the vows that he made to his wife. Still, he will continue to keep up appearances in order to avoid taking responsibility for "changing his mind" about the woman he married. More than likely, no one is forcing him to stay married. Although he may not admit it, he chooses to be where he is regardless of whatever feelings he claims to have for you. Aside from gaining an understanding of the lengths to which some men will go to perpetuate a fraudulent relationship, gaining first hand knowledge of the negative effects that mind killers have on relationships, and perhaps experiencing uninhibited sexual expression, there is little to be achieved by having an affair with a married man.

Several years ago, then-President of the United States Jimmy Carter confessed in an interview with *Playboy* magazine that he had "lusted in his heart" for women other than Mrs. Carter. That confession tarnished his squeaky clean personal image as an American role model. Needless to say, his confession was not well received by the American people. In essence, Mr. Carter was admitting to the *probability* of being unfaithful to his wife. He was also revealing the only "acceptable" form of adultery that a married person in America can commit. Providing of course that his lust was contained to the borders of his heart and not acted out. Mr. Carter admitted to committing an emotional infidelity against his wife. While he did not refer to his lust in any extreme, his confession implied a preoccupation with the possibility of committing a physical infidelity. Simply put, an emotional infidelity occurs when a man's thoughts are devoted to his desires for intimacy with a person other than his wife.

It is perfectly normal and healthy for a man to have thoughts of a sexual nature about other women. However, when a husband's attention shifts drastically from his marital routine to fantasies about other women, the potential for marital difficulties can increase. Comparatively speaking, an emotional infidelity is nothing like a physical infidelity. An emotional infidelity does not require that anything sexual actually happen. It is the idea that it could happen that makes it such an irresistible narcotic for some men. A husband who is unfortunate enough to succumb to this form of infidelity constantly dwells on "what ifs" and can be completely distracted by the possibility of an extramarital affair occurring. On the surface it might appear as though a man who cheats only in his mind is committing no offense. However, because he is allowing his mental love affair to dominate his thinking, his marriage is bound to suffer.

An emotional infidelity is an extremely cerebral experience that can occur when a married man's needs clash with his desires. Most married men can accept that their needs and their desires may be opposite extremes of their emotional makeup. If they can accept that, they create a system of checks and balances to help them cope with those desires that are thought to be counterproductive to their marital relationship. In other words, they teach themselves to want what they need and need what they want. Successfully married men seem to be able to allow their needs to dominate their desires.

SELF-SURVEY
IS THIS THE RIGHT MAN
FOR ME?

1. I have secret male friends because my husband/boyfriend is very jealous.

2. My husband/boyfriend doesn't spend a lot of time with me, but he buys me whatever I want.

3. My husband/boyfriend plays a key role in the positive feelings that I have about myself.

4. I can discuss my most intimate thoughts and feelings with my husband/boyfriend.

5. My husband/boyfriend doesn't want me to work. He says that he can give me everything that I need.

6. I make more money than my husband/boyfriend, but he doesn't seem to be bothered by that.

7. When my husband/boyfriend is unhappy, he takes it out on me until I'm just as unhappy as he is.

8. My husband/boyfriend is very close to his family. So, I do whatever it takes to stay in his good graces. Even if I don't want to.

9. My husband/boyfriend doesn't satisfy me sexually and doesn't want to talk with me about his performance in bed. So, I have a satisfying lover on the side.

10. I don't like waiting on my husband/boyfriend hand and foot, but if I don't, he makes me feel guilty.

156

CHAPTER SIX

Making Your Life Easier

Act through nonaction,
handle affairs through noninterference,
taste what has no taste,
regard the small things as great, the few as many,
repay resentment with integrity.
Undertake difficult tasks
by approaching what is simple in them.
Do great deeds
by focusing on their minute aspects.
All difficulties under heaven arise from what is easy.
All great things under heaven arise from what is minute.

For the Black woman in America, "life ain't no crystal stairs." Although her race, gender, and (sometimes) age are considered by some to be handicaps, it would be hard to imagine this world without her. Some of the most beautiful women in the world are and were Black Americans or persons of African descent. Eartha Kitt, Cleopatra, Josephine Baker, and Nefertiti are but a few. Some of the most brilliant legal and scientific minds belong to Black women. That includes, but is certainly not limited to, physicist Shirley

Ann Jackson, lawyer/ambassador Jewel Stradford Lafontant, astronaut/physician Mae C. Jemison and chemist/anthropologist Eslanda Goode Robeson. Some of the most courageous hearts beat strongly in the chests of Black women such as civil rights activists Attallah Shabazz and Coretta Scott King. In a world of few absolutes, you can be absolutely sure of who you are, where you belong, and what you can contribute. You can also be sure that whether you were born impoverished or privileged, there will always be someone somewhere who will be prejudiced against you because of the color of your skin. The history of Black Americans is filled with examples of that. However, you can still love yourself. Perhaps by demonstrating a love for yourself, your heritage, and your history others may try to love you too. Demonstrating self-love, you may also help others to look beyond the color of your skin and concentrate more on the content of your character. Try to remember the lessons you have learned throughout your growth process. That combined with your instinctive knowledge will help guide you towards a standard of excellence that is right for you.

GETTING RID OF THE BAD STUFF

When you hear the word "power," what comes to mind? Your first thoughts should be of yourself. However, if you are like most people, acknowledging your own power first is not an automatic response. Most people have learned to assign power and its qualities to things or to other people. For instance, a car that is big enough, fast enough, and equipped enough to take you anywhere you want to go would be considered powerful. A "state of the art" machine with seemingly unlimited life saving or life threatening capabilities is considered powerful. An individual who is muscular or physically strong enough to avenge or defend others or who is wise and crafty enough to manipulate circumstances is considered to be a powerful person.

Generally, Black people sabotage their own empowerment in two ways. First, they do not recognize their own power first. That is, they do not declare their own power before assigning it to things or to other people. Second, they limit their appreciation of power only to those things that can be detected by the five senses. They place more faith in the validity of their physical faculties than in their psychic and intuitive powers. For you, all things are possible. It is faith in possibilities that have compelled many Black Americans to fight for their ideals and challenge the system. While some people are content with waiting for the other guy to make the first move, only action will transform possibilities into realities. Just ask any successful entrepreneur, corporate CEO, first-time home buyer, or college graduate. These people know first hand that you have to be willing to do more than talk in order to reach whatever your idea of success is. While it is certainly an undeniable reality, racism does not prevent you from reaching your goals. Only you have the power to do that. Getting rid of the bad stuff like fear, complacency, ignorance, and uncontrolled anger is an ongoing process. You should expect to deal with them many times during your life. Getting rid of them happens when you accept not only that something greater than yourself exists, but that you are a part of that greatness!

LIFE'S 7 GOLDEN RULES

Rules are "necessary evils" in this society. They are tools that we can use to help us maintain reasonable control over ourselves and sometimes over other people. Control will always be warranted because not everyone has learned how to exist peacefully with other people. The rules that govern you should assist you in remaining unencumbered as you pursue your goals. Their ultimate purpose is to pave the way for the most positive experiences that this life can offer.

Rule #1: Acknowledge your motives.

You may choose to play games with others, but don't play them with yourself. Your motives for the pursuit of any goal need to be clear in your mind first. Other people will scrutinize you as long as your actions go against the status quo. However, why you are doing whatever you are doing should not be an unanswered question for you.

Only you can put limits on the degrees to which your needs and desires extend themselves. No one else has the power or right to do that. Resolving of your basic needs is your responsibility. You can meet that responsibility without infringing on the rights of other people. Motives are what cause us to take action. For example, suppose that you needed money. That need might motivate you to look for a job. If money were the only motive that you chose to deal with, you would take a job anywhere. However, if you are also motivated to maintain a sense of status you might limit your employment choices. For example, Jane is a Black woman who is admittedly ambitious and assertive. Her goal is to acquire money and all of the prestige that comes with it. She has made it clear that she will do anything to get ahead. Even exchange sexual favors. She is so motivated to achieve her definition of success that she chooses not to consider herself as being exploited. In this example, the motives are clear.

There is no reason for you to be motivated by the same things as everyone else. However, if you do not acknowledge your true motives of operation (at least to yourself), you run the risk of being exploited by other people. As long as you can accept your motives, that is what's most important. You have to be able to live with yourself and with the decisions that you make in your lifetime. Remember that you always have a choice. There are always alternatives. It is through recognizing and exercising those alternatives that allows you to maintain a sense of control over your life. You are responsible for the choices that you make. Even if no one else is aware of the reasons for your actions, you must be. That knowledge will prevent others from manipulating you.

Rule #2: Never mix business with pleasure.

It will be in your best interest to avoid playing where you work or working where you play. Even though situations may arise during your lifetime that will attract, intrigue, and seduce you, working where you play and playing where you work should not be one of them. Generally, business matters do not blend well with personal ones. The nature of business is cold and unemotional. It does not accommodate emotionalism. Romance on the job is a good example. There can be any number of reasons why a relationship of this nature should not interest you. It is highly unlikely that those who work with you will be unaware of what's going on, even though they will probably not say anything to your face. Office romances have a way of leaking out sooner or later. Even if both of you deny it to coworkers, they will no doubt be alerted to the truth by the changes in your body language, temperament, and general disposition, no matter how strongly you protest.

This rule not only applies to your male coworkers. It is just as applicable to your female coworkers. Generally, females tend to be less willing to control their emotional distresses and can be easily distracted by events that upset their sense of emotional balance. Typically, if a female coworker is upset with you, she will not confront you directly. Instead, she will engage in avoidance games such as ignoring you or selective forgetfulness about directives you may have given to her.

If you choose to develop a personal relationship and/or friendship at work, you must realize that if your basic personalities are not compatible, your "friend" may not be able to separate the working relationship that you have from the personal one. If the female is a subordinate, your effectiveness as a director could be compromised by her inability or unwillingness to respect your position of authority. If you are a subordinate to her, you may be able to enjoy certain "privileges" while your association is amicable. However, if your friendship should become interrupted or severed, she may not be able to treat you fairly as a coworker or employee because of the emotions that she has invested in the friendship. Establishing a friendly atmosphere at work is always preferable to one that is hostile. Still, the work environment must support the basic philosophies of the business. The bottom line has to be that goals are attained as smoothly as possible. Your place of work should be unencumbered by scenarios that promote confusion, disloyalty, or disrespect.

Rule #3: Keep your enemies close to you.

In the real world, people will generally oppose or assist you. Those individuals who help you in order to help themselves will be numerous. Fortunately, they will probably also be transient with regards to your life path. There will also be those who will help you because they sense your capacity for greatness. Those persons are able to achieve

162

their own sense of worth vicariously by contributing to your pursuits of excellence. They will be thrilled to be a part of what they believe is eminent. Others will help you because of what you represent to them. For example, you may be thought of as a logical spokesperson for their cause or a worthy representative of their principles.

Those who oppose you may or may not do so openly. The motives of people who oppose you may be less obvious than those of persons who want to assist you. For all practical purposes, these people are your enemies. There can be any number of reasons for the oppositional stance that they have chosen. Not everyone will accept who you are. Not everyone will like who you are. Some people may become upset and resentful of the influence they believe that you have in their lives. Sometimes your enemies will make themselves known. Sometimes they will not. Your enemies will not always come to you in war paint and armor. A formidable adversary will come to you in the guise of a friend.

An enemy does not have to be a homicidal or deranged person. An enemy is anyone who is consciously motivated to impede your efforts or harm you in any way. The clerk who repeatedly "forgets" to deliver important material to your supervisors is your enemy. The switchboard operator who consistently refuses to direct telephone calls from influential clients to you is your enemy. They may be enemies on a small scale. They may be people who present only minor challenges to you, but they are still your enemies. Until they demonstrate a willingness to work with you and not against you, you should be aware of them There may be nothing that you can do to change their feelings about you, but it would be wise for you to try. At the very least, you may learn something about yourself in the process. Everyone can teach you something. Even your enemies. It is not paranoid to be cautious of others. As long as you do not overreact to every adverse event that happens, you will probably do well.

If you know who your enemies are, don't help them to destroy you by revealing your weaknesses. Develop the art of listening. It is a skill that will serve you well during your "battles." Learn all that you can as unobtrusively as possible. Be aware of the whereabouts of your enemies and their true roles in the game. If you can manipulate those roles in a positive way, it might be to your advantage to do so. Remember that your enemies can only harm you if you allow them to.

Rule #4: Know when to quit.

None of us enjoys the taste of failure. We would rather dine on the spoils of success. Knowing when to say "when" can actually make the difference between success and failure. Before you pursue any goal, do your homework. Find out how much time, money, and effort it will take to meet your objectives. Most of us have an ample supply of hindsight that enables us to look back on our experiences and pinpoint errors. Few people are able to exercise enough foresight to prevent a waste of time and energy from occurring. If you have fully analyzed your goals and have designed a sophisticated enough strategy, you may be able to overcome many factors that might interfere with meeting your goals. You may also be able to avoid "overkill" by making certain that the goals you set are worth the effort it will take to reach them.

It doesn't matter what the goal is. Let us suppose that your goal is to attend a postgraduate studies program at your local university. First of all, is your goal realistic? Do you clearly have the aptitude to succeed through the curriculum? If so, have you fulfilled all of the necessary academic requirements? If not, how much time will it take for you to do that? Is the pursuit of your goal economically feasible? Will the pursuing of it jeopardize your ability to support yourself or your family? If everything does not balance out for you, then you may need to modify your strategy.

Take the road of least resistance. It would be illogical for you to remain on a path that stifles your progress. It would also be unwise to allow yourself to become so passionate about your goals that you are blind to the obvious deterrents to achieving them. You could also hamper your progress by being so protective of your game plan that you are unwilling to modify it. Stay focused on your goal, but leave room for the possibility of a change in direction. You may even have to postpone your pursuits. Every factor that might influence your pursuits won't be under your direct control or even of your own doing. There is a lot that can be said for timing. In all cases, timing is everything.

Rule #5: Avoid making the same mistake twice.

You will always have a tremendous capacity for learning as long as you open yourself up to being taught. The quality that makes ignorant people ignorant is not what they don't know, but what they refuse to learn. Your life will be a series of lessons. Some of those lessons will confirm your beliefs in the basic nature of people. Others will challenge them. Your lessons will not always be pleasant and painless, but they will all be *essential* to your personal growth. Recognize those experiences as lessons and allow yourself to grow from them. As those lessons are brought to you, you should change your patterns of thinking and behaving. If you have truly learned each lesson, a change in you will happen.

When you accept life's experiences as lessons, change will be the result. You cannot base the changes you make on the way that other people might behave if placed in the same situation. No two people see the same thing in exactly the same way. So, someone else might react to that same situation in an entirely different way. In the spiritual sense, a lifetime is a blink of an eye with respect to "the big picture." You have no knowledge of how your decisions will affect the remainder of your life because the big picture is not something that is privy to your wisdom. For that reason, the decisions that you make should be made with life lessons in mind.

This does not mean that you should judge a person solely on the basis of past experiences. It also does not mean that you should abandon what you know to be human nature, either. Although each person is unique, few people are without some measure of predictability. For instance, if a person is given the choice of either telling the truth or telling a lie, you can make a fairly accurate prediction of which choice will be made based on what you have learned from your past experiences.

For the most part, people are motivated by fear to tell lies. They will lie if they are afraid that the truth will harm them in any way. Since we are all creatures of comfort, we don't like to be uncomfortable about anything. We especially don't like to be uncomfortable about ourselves. In order for some people to maintain their comfort levels, they tell lies. A lie is how some people cope with their anxieties. The choice of telling a lie and telling the truth will depend on an individual's ability to control his/her fears. People who work towards mastering their fears will tend not to lie because they recognize that they have nothing (of real value) to lose by telling the truth.

As you grow, you will learn to hold on to those experiences that contributed to your growth. Even the painful, confusing, and uncomfortable ones. Your lifetime will offer countless opportunities for mistakes to occur. Those mistakes won't always be made by you. The people in your personal and professional life will make their share of mistakes, too. It doesn't matter who makes the mistake. What matters is that you learn from the mistake. The moment that it is made, by whomever makes it, the opportunity for learning will present itself to you. Recognize that moment.

Rule #6: *Beware of the love of money.*

You have no doubt heard the saying "money is the root of all evil." Actually, the statement is a partial paraphrase from the Bible. The complete scripture reads: "The love of money is the root of all evil." As you can see, there is a huge difference between the two statements. Still, there are some people who attach a degree of "sin" to having money. In reality, it is not money, but the love of it that motivates people to "sin against" other people.

America is a totally profit-driven country. Money is held in high reverence here. To Americans, money is power, and power over others is everything. Money is so worshipped that persons who possess large quantities of it secure the privileges of deities. Those without it may do anything to get it. Those with it may do anything to keep it. The ascribed power that money has over most people is nothing short of amazing. Having it is a criteria for every form of social interaction that occurs between people. While it is true that money cannot buy love in the spiritual sense, it can most certainly buy large quantities of physical love. Money cannot return a life that has ended, but it can definitely improve the quality of living. However, money alone cannot make you into what you're not. It can only magnify what you are. That is, if you are a good person, money will make you into a better one. If you are a bad person, money will make you into an even worse person. If you're an addict, money only will make you a rich addict. If you're a humanitarian, money will only make you a philanthropic humanitarian.

For many Black Americans, money remains an elusive commodity. Money is something that too many Black people only dream of obtaining. The proverbial "silver spoon" rarely lands on the palates of Black children at birth. Those Black persons who are industrious enough to obtain it are frequently left to their own devices and must often invent their own means of sustaining their wealth. Throughout your growth process you will see countless examples of what Black people will do to acquire and accumulate money. The more motivated they are to have it, the more energy they will put into getting it. Those people who are satisfied with having enough money to maintain a "simple" lifestyle will only invest enough energy to maintain that standard of living. On the other hand, people who aspire to achieve what they believe to be "the good life" will be much more aggressive in their pursuits of it.

Some people will choose to acquire money through entrepreneurial pursuits. Others less willing to devote the time and effort to such endeavors may try to obtain it vicariously. That is, through associations with others who have it.

In reality, *the only real power that money has is the power that you assign to it.* This society has ensured that the survival level of its people rests with the amount of money that they can obtain. Respect money. It can bring out the best in us. It can also bring out the worst in us. Money can divide or unite us. It can be wonderful or terrible. While capitalism reigns in America, there will be few things of earthly value that money cannot buy. Money is the tool of the ruling forces in this country. Recognize that fact.

Rule #7: Take care of your body.

As you pursue your goals, your physical well being will be just as important as your mental well being. You will need to be actively involved in your physical fitness and general health. No matter what your age, you are responsible for the general condition that your body is in. After all, your body is the vehicle through which your goals are met. It must be ready to meet the demands that reaching your goals require. There may be plenty of days when your work schedule won't permit you to take an extended lunch break. This does not mean that you should ignore good nutrition.

168

As difficult as it might be to maintain a balanced diet, doing so will help you to ward off medical complications that can seriously affect your ability to perform. Your attention to good nutrition will also help you to control your body weight.

It goes without saying that you will need to be in complete control of your faculties during every phase of your pursuits. So, drugs and alcohol are out. Drugs and alcohol will impair your judgment and slow your responses. Avoid them. Under no circumstances should you combine alcohol with business. Leave the "liquid lunches" alone. If you do drink alcohol, try to keep your indulgences in moderation. Above all, never, ever drink and drive, not even for short distances. Even a little "buzz" can cause you to make grave errors in driving judgment. Use common sense.

A well-rested body will make the difference in your ability to function at your optimum. So, try to get the amount of rest that you need. Sleep deprivation can have serious side effects that you might not recognize until it is too late. Not everyone has the same sleep requirements. Try to adhere to whatever your body needs for sleep. Don't wait for your body to start pleading with you for relief. Learn how to pace yourself.

Your fitness would not be complete without attention to exercise. You are no doubt familiar with the reported benefits of regular exercise. We can't all be a size six (and may not want to be), but we can all profit from regular exercise. Aside from the cosmetic benefits, regular exercise will help to improve the quality of your life. Make time for exercise. A few hours a week devoted to brisk walking, biking, swimming, or weight training will make a tremendous difference in how you look and feel. That difference can translate into success for you.

THE POWER OF PRAYER, POSITIVE THINKING, AND AFFIRMATIONS

Strength is not just a matter of extensive territory
and large population,
victory is not just a matter of efficient armaments,
security is not just a matter of high walls
and deep moats,
authority is not just a matter of strict orders
and frequent punishments.
Those who establish viable organization
will survive even if they are small,
while those who establish a moribund organization
will perish even if they are large.

Nothing moves us like prayer. Nothing inspires us like our faith in an All Mighty being. Even those who choose not to endorse any religious belief can be overwhelmed by the acts of faith shown by others. For some of us, prayer is all inclusive. Prayer is holistic. It encompasses everything that we do, see, and are. For others, the impact that prayer has on our lives is taken for granted. For any number of reasons, prayer has become something that is done so habitually that the real meaning behind the act is lost. Still others dismiss prayer as illogical and denounce the authenticity of its power. Whether we grow up to be adults who accept atheism, religious fanaticism, religious conservatism, religious liberalism, or agnosticism depends largely on how our early beliefs were shaped.

As children we are little more than ego-centered small people. We view the entire world in accordance with the satisfaction of our own needs. During the earliest stages of our lifespan, we believe that *everything* revolves around us. It is only when we demonstrate a willingness to give of ourselves that the first signs of maturity can be affirmed. Until such time, we are concerned only with our place in the universe, which we most certainly perceive as centering around us. Unless we are reared by people who maintain a strict "orthodox" religious view or literal religious posture, our views of religion and prayer might often take a back seat to our earthly concerns.

It might be difficult for many adults to remember their first introduction to religion. Religious teachings tend to be specific to individual cultures. Your initial exposure to it could have ranged from attending church services with family and friends to participating in church-sponsored food drives for the needy. Regardless of what specific experiences occurred, some part of our personal history includes childhood experiences that prompted our total acceptance (or rejection) *as fact* of someone who could not be seen, physically touched, or engaged with in a two-sided conversation who could have such a profound influence over our lives. That acceptance is what we call "faith." It is not something that is tangible. It is not something that is purely logical or something that one person can force another person to accept.

Faith comes from within. It is not something that you acquire on the basis of intelligence, race, or wealth. The fact that it is so indescribable and intangible makes it all the more difficult to communicate. However, conveying your sense of faith to a child can be made easier through prayer. Praying is a concrete and identifiable activity in which a child can be taught to engage. Teaching prayer to your children is a personal choice that only you can make. Doing so may not instill in them *your* degree of faith, but the tools that you use to teach prayer to them can serve to alert them to their own mortality as well as assure them of their own personal power. Only you can decide when and if your children are ready for that experience. Amazingly, at a time when a person is most self-centered and self-absorbed, s/he can be guided to accept that someone greater than him/her exists.

171

Prayer is a wonderful way for us to make the spiritual connections that many of us need to feel complete. Unfortunately for some of us, prayer has become an act of desperation, a synonym for wishing. It has become something for people to turn to when faith in their own abilities is lost. Some people pray for relief from personal pain, change from an intolerable situation, or an increase in personal wealth as they approach a low point in their lives. No matter how earnest their prayers seem to be, they are usually laced with an edge of disbelief that those prayers will not be "answered." We learn how to pray and to whom to pray very early in life, but many of us do not learn how to affirm ourselves in the process. When we use prayer without affirmation, we are simply engaging in a stylized form of wishing that does not allow for the personal power we all possess.

Recognizing your own personal power is an important ability that many people do not seem to possess. For instance, a man who has lost his job may opt to pray for employment. He may do this without even considering the possibility that his unemployment may very well contribute to his personal growth in some way. Instead of upgrading his job skills, taking a more original approach to finding another job, or pursuing his dream of being a self-employed person, he chooses to place his faith in someone that he believes is more powerful than he is. He chooses to believe that what a "higher power" can do for him is more than what he can do for himself. He chooses to rely on supernatural intervention to change his situation instead of his ability to intervene in the course of his own affairs.

It is so easy for some people to accept that ultimate control of their lives is not in their hands. There may always be people who allow the faith that they have in their God to strip them of their ability to see themselves as powerful forces and controllers of their destinies. It is not their faith in God that is damaging. It is their lack of faith in themselves. Instead of utilizing their inner strength and good-

172

ness, they become dependent on the strength and goodness of others. The decision to assume such a passive posture allows them to view themselves as victims and pawns. This way they can blame their misfortunes on Divine Will or credit their accomplishments to Holy Grace. So much of the human spirit is lost when we ignore our human possibilities. Faith in God inspires supreme love and indescribable joy. As long as God lives within you, all things are possible. In recognizing His/Her Goodness and power, you are seeing what is inherently good and powerful in you.

When you acknowledge your belief in a Supreme Being, you are also acknowledging your own mortality. Still, coming to terms with your human limitations does not mean ignoring your own spiritual power. It does not matter whether you pray to God, Allah, Jesus, Buddah, or any other divine figure. What matters most is that you do view yourself as ineffective when you pray. Your prayers of thanks and for enlightenment can be delivered with the knowledge that you possess free will and are ultimately accountable for the choices *that you make*

By definition, praying requires that we assume a humble posture, shed our self-pride, and place the faith that we have in ourselves *secondary* to our faith in the spiritual powers of the being(s) that we pray to. In the literal sense, we are in no way assertive when we pray and tend to accept that assertiveness on our part would be inappropriate. We stylize our petitions to God and make our requests to Him/Her in the form of a plea. A literal interpretation of praying directs us to "place ourselves in His/Her hands." Generally, when all possible options seem to have been exhausted, it is time to pray. When there seems to be no end in sight to our misfortunes, it is time to pray. Whenever we are overwhelmed by our own accomplishments, it is time to offer a prayer of thanks. Whenever we cannot understand or reconcile the death of a loved one, it is time to express our sorrow in the form of a prayer. Whenever we believe that we have "taken" as much as we can tolerate, it is time to pray for relief.

Sometimes what we do not stop to consider is that praying alone is only one step in a series of steps that contribute to spiritual power and awareness. Although it is a wonderful first step, it is not the only step that needs to be taken. Some of us view praying as a passive, one-sided experience. Maintaining that point of view proposes that religious faith is a valid reason to deny personal power and ultimate responsibility for individual choices. For instance, if denied a much-deserved job promotion, you might accept such a denial as "God's will." If faced with an unexpected reward, you might accept the unorthodox nature of the gift as an example of God's mysterious working ways. If plagued by a series of mishaps, you might accept those occurrences as Divine tests of worthiness. If you have incorporated your religious beliefs into your daily living, your prayers might address these issues. If you take a literal approach to your prayer offerings, you might be cheating yourself out of the full benefits of spiritual enlightenment.

On the other hand, a person who combines prayer with affirmations is as spiritually uplifted (if not more so) as the person who has turned only to prayer. An important difference between prayer and self-affirmations is that self-affirmations encourage a person to call upon the courage and strength from within to resolve situations or realize their potential.

An affirmation is not a plea. It is a declaration. It is as solemn as a prayer, but it cannot replace prayer and cannot be truly made without a sincere belief in divine forces. Affirmations are not meant to replace prayers. They are meant to supplement them. Both can help to bring you closer to your God. Both can be used in anticipation of or in the face of adversity. Both can be spiritually uplifting. However, affirmations allow you to focus on the personal and spiritual power that you already have. They help you to view yourself as a "master" of your own fate, controller of your own destiny, and ruler of your own life. Affirmations can help to change the perspective that you have of your life, your degree of power, and your ability to exert control.

For instance, a wife may discover that her husband is having an extramarital affair. She may seek spiritual comfort to help relieve her pain. If she chooses only to pray, those prayers might be that her husband be "made to" honor their vows, that she be "told" what she should do, or that she be "shown" the right way. If she chooses to include affirmations in her prayer ritual, she would not only be expressing her willingness to take full responsibility for her own happiness, but would also be freeing herself of the pain she associates with having to rely on someone else for it. A good affirmation in this case might be: "I have the courage to face the truth and be strengthened by it." She might also affirm that, "I will allow the pain that I experience today to teach and heal me." Affirmations are statements that center around actions that you will take. They will always include verbs like "can" and "will" to help you focus on being an active participant in your experiences.

There are many benefits to using affirmations. Namely, they guide you towards recognizing situations as they arise as well as your role in reinforcing those situations. They can help you to assume responsibility for your own actions as well as assist you in developing faith in your abilities. For example, "My yesterdays have prepared me for whatever comes today. I am ready"; and "If I feel trapped by my circumstances, I will first look at how I built the trap and then at how I can disassemble it" are two affirmations that can help you to concentrate on your abilities and assume a positive attitude about controlling your life. Even if you are not facing a dilemma or trying to solve a problem, affirmations like these can be an uplifting way to start your day: "I will remember that wishing without working towards my goal is not enough. I can make my wishes come true if I work at them." "Achieving my level of peace is my responsibility. Today I will be as happy as I want to be." "I will not be afraid of change. I trust that it will bring me unexpected growth." "I can achieve freedom when I choose self-control."

As you pray and affirm, keep in mind that as a Black woman you are the descendent of kings. The blood of monarchs courses through your veins. As a Black woman, you are kin to some of the greatest scientific, mathematical, artistic, and medical minds that the world has ever known. You need bow to no one. Nor should you allow yourself to be defeated by the fears of other people, even when those fears take the form of prejudice and discrimination against you. Maintain your faith in your God-given rights. Conduct yourself with the utmost pride in your heritage with the level of dignity befitting all Black women. Rather than be a carrier of ill will, choose to be a messenger of good news.

ACHIEVING PERSONAL PEACE

Therefore those who win every battle
are not really skillful.
Those who render others' armies helpless
without fighting are the best of all.

If you are not at peace with yourself and with the person that you have grown to become, the negative actions of others will have more of an affect on you than on someone who is reconciled with him/herself. Being at peace with yourself is a state of mind that is achieved through successfully balancing the emotional opposites that make us human. Opposites like right and wrong, kindness and cruelty, masculinity and femininity, and generosity and selfishness exist to help make us complete. When you are at peace with yourself, you are far from being a perfect person. What inner peace does is allow you to accept your place in the universe. It allows you to recognize your human faults and be willing to put forth the effort to overcome them. When you are at peace with yourself, you are able to maintain a level of inner spiritual strength. That strength is held "in reserve" and available to you at will to ward off the negative impulses of mind killers that occur in all of us at some time in our lives.

Being at peace with yourself implies that you have faith in the divine will that dictates the outcome of "the big picture." Being at peace with yourself means that you fully recognize your human weaknesses without being overly concerned by them. It means consciously acknowledging your strengths without being overly impressed by them. Being at peace with yourself means that you maintain a realistic view of yourself that includes an accurate balance of optimism and pessimism.

Being at peace is something that you must "program"

yourself to maintain. It can take many years for that process to be completed. We can begin that process by examining the world on a simplified level. Especially our comforts and discomforts. If we allow the attitudes of those people around us to be filtered into our way of thinking, it will be they, not us, who define our definitions of peace of mind. For example, consider the mind killer: uncontrolled anger. It may not seem possible to most people, but uncontrolled anger like any other mind killer is a chosen attitude. Although it is just as easy to reject it, uncontrolled anger often serves as a convenient and automatic solution to situations in life that do not comply with our desires. Think for a moment about the driver on route to work who gets caught in a traffic jam. Instead of being thankful for having a job or having the transportation to get there, s/he becomes uncontrollably angry over the delay. Like other mind killers, uncontrolled anger is a learned response.

Throughout our lives people have taught us to use anger to achieve our immediate goals. For example, as toddlers, adolescents, or teens we learned how to express our anger over our unmet desires through the use of physical aggression, temper tantrums, or words that hurt. The child who does not share his/her toys with playmates and is not convinced of the importance of sharing can become an adult who lacks the ability to be compassionate towards others. The child who succeeds in arousing the uncontrolled parental anger that precedes the "spanking" may eventually learn two things. If the spankings occur frequently enough, the child first learns (how) to hold on to his anger. S/he learns to keep angry feelings hidden in order to avoid the spanking. The spanking eventually becomes a symbolic gesture that teaches the child his second lesson, which is, how to use his anger against others. He learns (through his experiences with parental discipline) to vent his anger against those persons over which he can dominate. A child's experience with uncontrolled adult anger can teach him to either internalize his anger or express it in physically violent ways.

Positive communication between parents, care givers, and adults is crucial to healthy child development. It shouldn't take a child psychologist or pediatric specialist to recognize that how we communicate with one another is just as important to healthy development as what we communicate. You can learn to express your disapproval of anything in a positive way. The expression of your anger does not have to be forceful or threatening. Disapproval of anything can be expressed in a calm and reasonable fashion if you choose to do it. If you allow the stresses of modern living to rob you of the ability to peacefully resolve differences, you run the risk of doing irreversible damage to everyone around you. When we choose to violently disagree with one another instead of amicably working towards a solution, they negatively influence another person's view of us.

Remember that we are the sum of our experiences. That is why our childhood experiences have such an impact on the adults who we are. Children who witness parental feuding run the risk of becoming adults who resort to relying on uncontrolled anger to resolve disputes. The male child who learns aggression from a physically abusive father is also learning to become a wife beater himself. The female child who learns passivity from an abused mother is also learning how to become a victim. Adults are the sum total of their childhood experiences.

How we resolve our adult differences serves as the groundwork for how our children learn to resolve their differences. Children by nature will role play, copy, mock, and parrot those things that intrigue them. Naturally adults are the prime targets of their immature curiosity. As adults, we are the models for what they may become. They are constantly seeking to absorb information from us. They hold on to the images that adults provide. They translate those adult behaviors into simplistic terms that they can digest as children. Once that is achieved, that information is stored for use later. All too often that information resurfaces in them as adults. Sometimes adults forget that children are very susceptible to all of the negative (as well as positive) forces that surround them. They hear what we think has been whispered. They see what we think has been camouflaged. They acknowledge what we think has been omitted. They sense what we think has been concealed. Children are acutely aware of our anger even when we think we are being subtle. They have an uncanny ability to detect those changes in our touch, in our eyes, and in the tone of our speech that signal to them that something is not "right."

If the expression of your anger compels you to be outwardly abusive, you establish patterns that ensnare your children and teach them to become abusive adults. The child who is abused can easily become the adult who (in turn) abuses. As adults we must find ways to manage our anger. Not deny or displace it, but manage it. We can deal with our anger responsibly. We can learn to channel our anger in positive ways. We can learn that there are alternative ways to violent outbursts and arguments. We do not have to resort to hurting one another in order to relieve our frustrations. We are all capable of engaging in healthy and positive dialogues with our coworkers, friends, family members, and our children. Our peace of mind depends on it.

SELF-SURVEY #6
AM I MAKING MY LIFE HARDER THAN IT HAS TO BE?

1. There's nothing wrong with wanting to be rich as long as you don't kill yourself trying to do it.

2. If I work hard enough, sooner or later someone's bound to appreciate it.

3. I do most things my way

4. I don't believe in hunches. If you can't see it, then it isn't real.

5. When I make a decision, it's final.

6. I can be diplomatic as long as I get what I want in the end.

7. If something sounds too good to be true, it usually is.

8. I always take the time to "read the fine print" when I get into a situation.

9. Most of the time my focus is on what's probable. Not on what's possible.

10. A person will change if you offer the right motivation.

Bibliography

Burt, M. *Black Inventors of America.* Oregon: National Book Company, 1989.

Chissell, J. T. *Pyramids of Power!* Baltimore: Positive Perceptions Publications, 1993.

Covey, S. R. *The 7 Habits of Highly Effective People.* New York: Simon and Schuster, 1989.

Fisher, H. E., "After All, Maybe It's Biology." *Psychology Today,* 1993 pp. 40-45

Hay, L. L. *Heal Your Body.* California: Hay House, Incorporated, 1982.

Helms, D. B. and J. S. Turner *Life Span Development.* Florida: Holt, Rinehart and Winston, Incorporated, 1991.

Lanker, B. *I Dream a World: Portraits of Black Women Who Changed America.* New York: Stewart, Tabori & Chang, 1989.

Margolis, L. and D. Sagan. *Mystery Dance: On the Evolution of Human Sexuality.* New York: Summit Books, 1991.

Smith, J. C. *Epic Lives: One Hundred Black Women Who Made a Difference.* Michigan: Visible Ink Press, 1993.

Tzu, Lao. *Tao Te Ching: The Classic Book of Integrity and the Way.* New York: Bantam Books, 1990.

Tzu, Sun *The Art of War.* Massachusetts: Shambhala Publications, Incorporated, 1988.